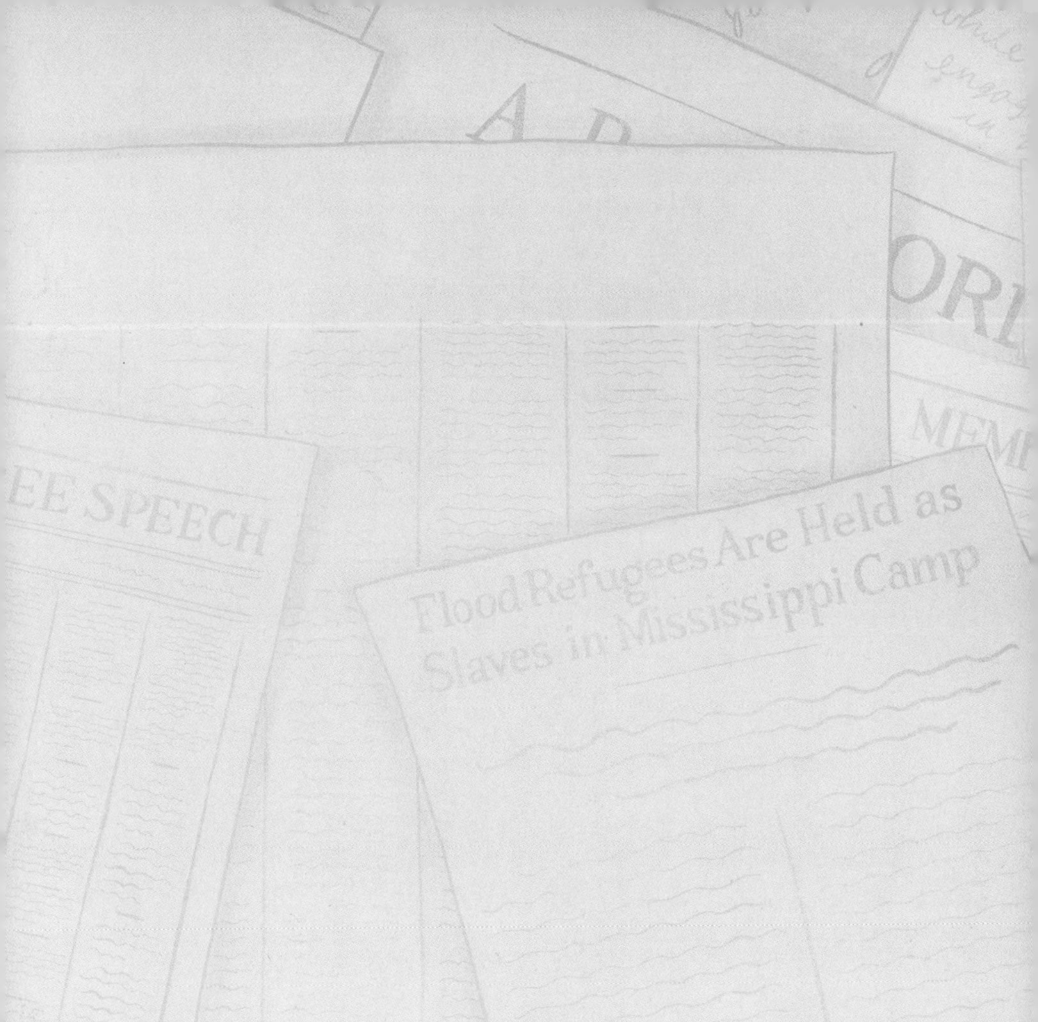
EE SPEECH
Flood Refugees Are Held as
Slaves in Mississippi Camp

8501 West Higgins Road
Chicago, Illinois 60631

59 Gloucester Place
London W1U 8JJ

Heimhuder Straße 81
20148 Hamburg

www.sunbirdkidsbooks.com

Library of Congress Control Number: 2021936150

ISBN: 978-1-5037-6008-0 Printed in China

The art for this book was created digitally.
Text set in Superclarendon.

IT'S HER STORY

IDA B. WELLS

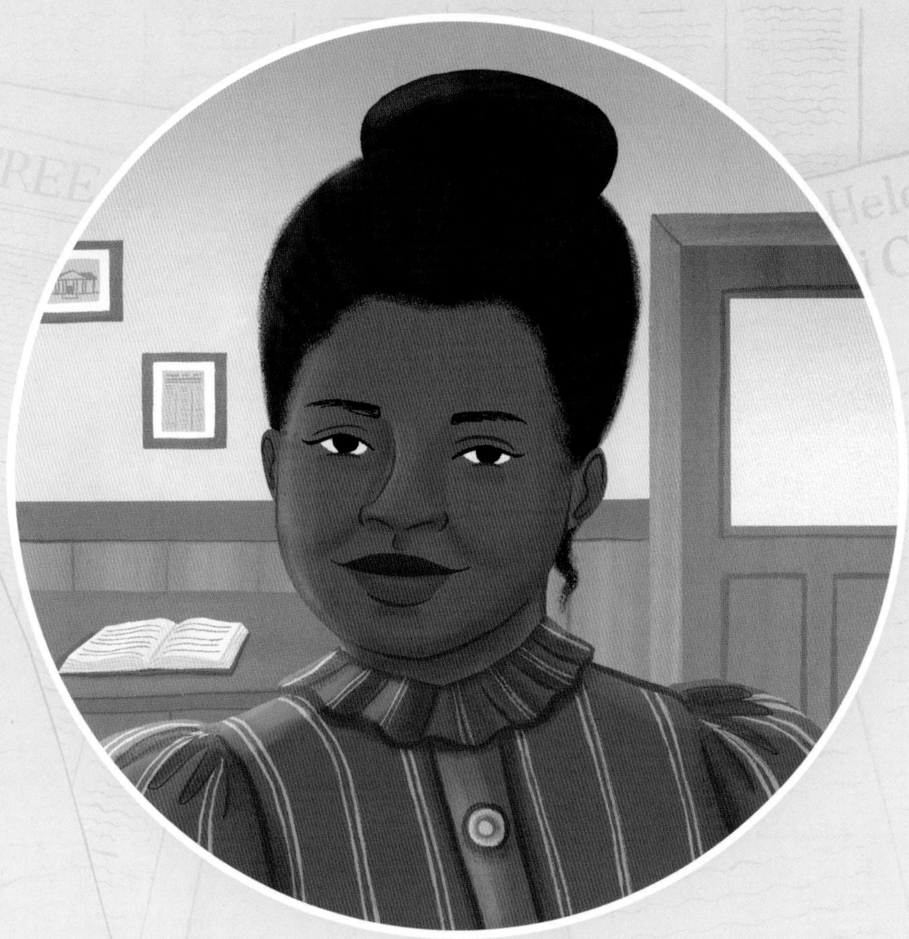

Written by Anastasia Magloire Williams
Illustrated by Alleanna Harris

sunbird books

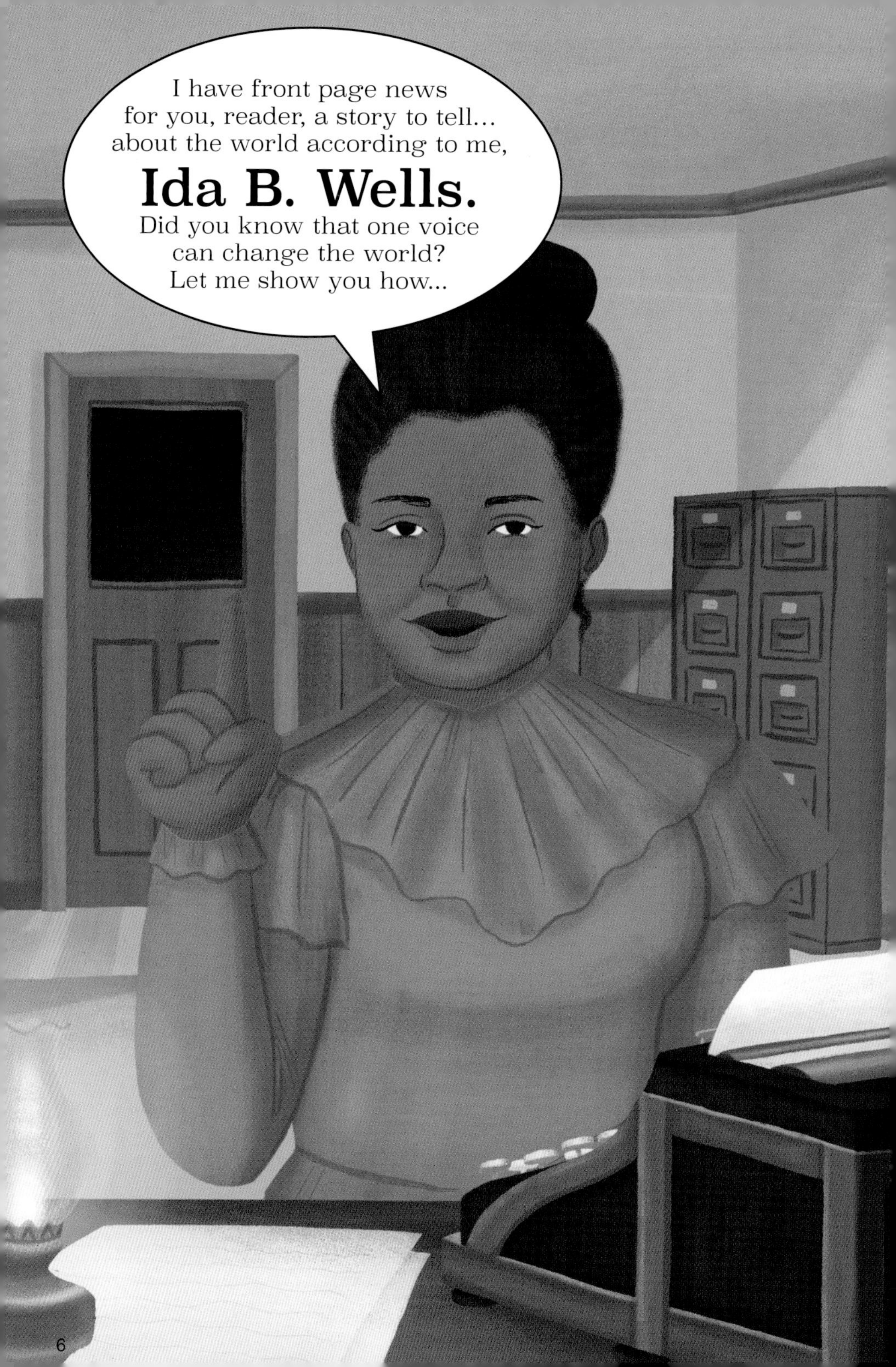
I have front page news
for you, reader, a story to tell...
about the world according to me,
Ida B. Wells.
Did you know that one voice
can change the world?
Let me show you how...

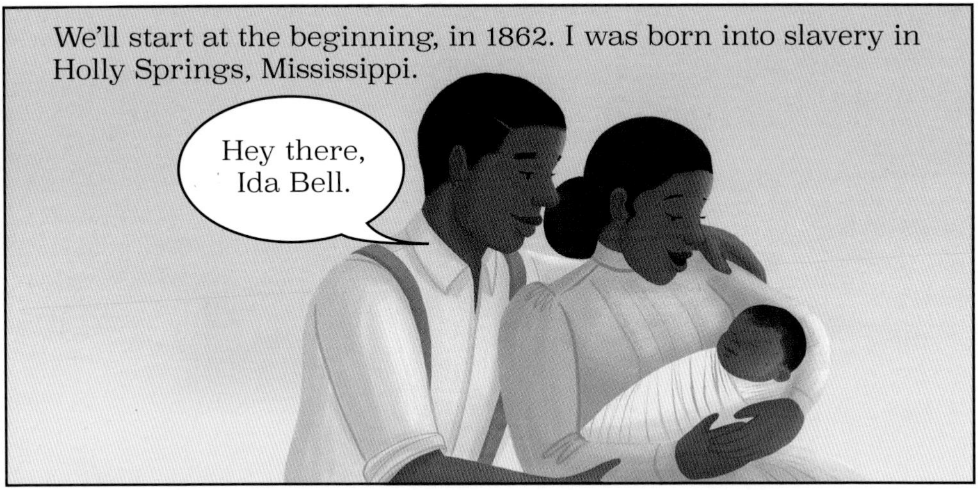
We'll start at the beginning, in 1862. I was born into slavery in Holly Springs, Mississippi.
Hey there, Ida Bell.

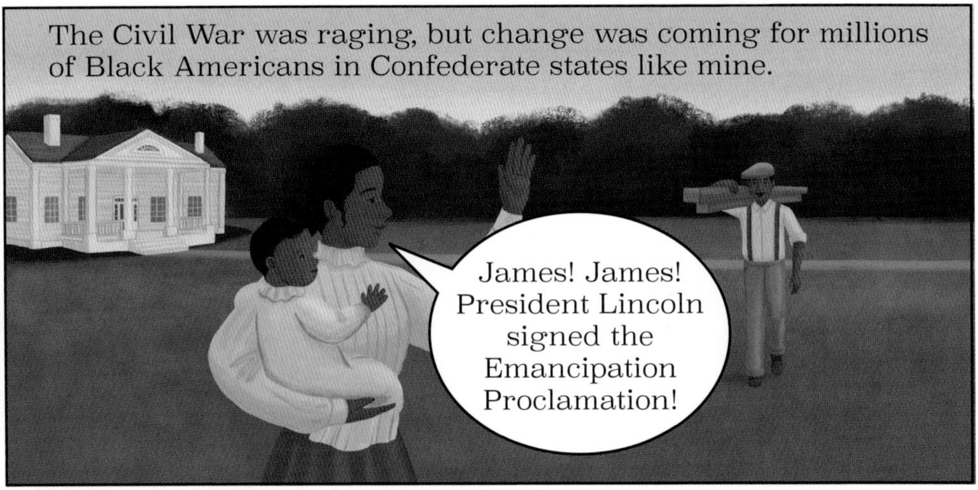
The Civil War was raging, but change was coming for millions of Black Americans in Confederate states like mine.
James! James! President Lincoln signed the Emancipation Proclamation!

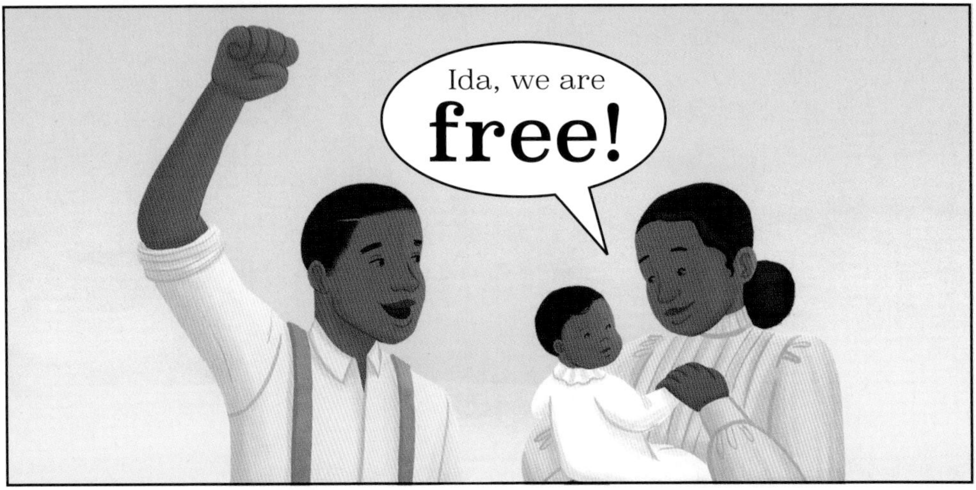
Ida, we are **free!**

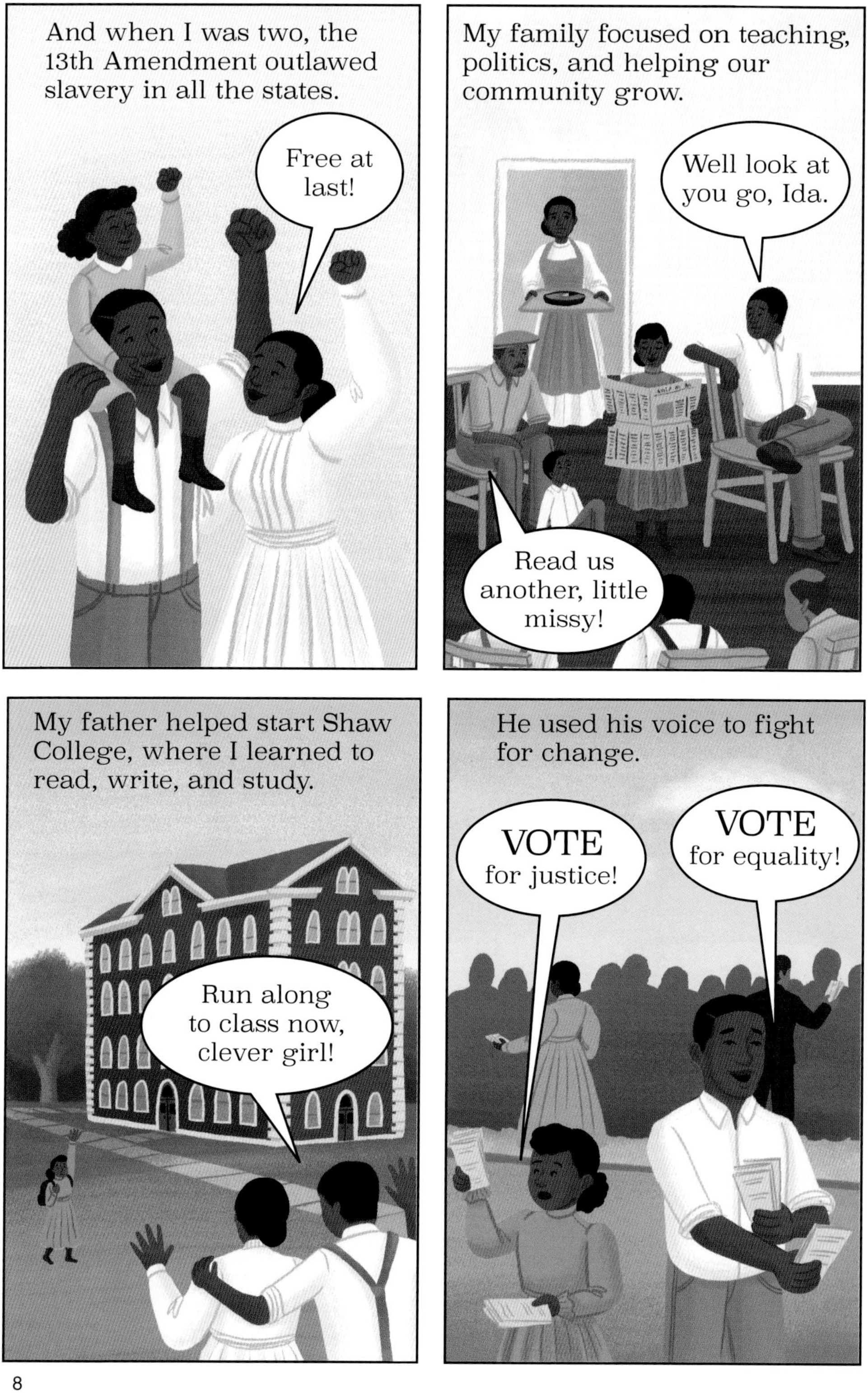
And when I was two, the 13th Amendment outlawed slavery in all the states.
Free at last!
My family focused on teaching, politics, and helping our community grow.
Well look at you go, Ida.
Read us another, little missy!
My father helped start Shaw College, where I learned to read, write, and study.
Run along to class now, clever girl!
He used his voice to fight for change.
VOTE for justice!
VOTE for equality!

But not all change is easy...

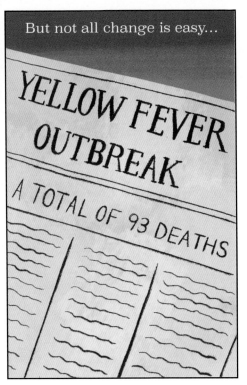

YELLOW FEVER OUTBREAK

A TOTAL OF 93 DEATHS

In 1878, when the fever came to Holly Springs, my parents and baby brother died.

I vowed to take care of my siblings. I was only 16, but I could teach.

Miss Ida! Miss Ida!

I was free to earn a living, pass down the lessons my parents had taught me, and help keep my family together.

Amen!

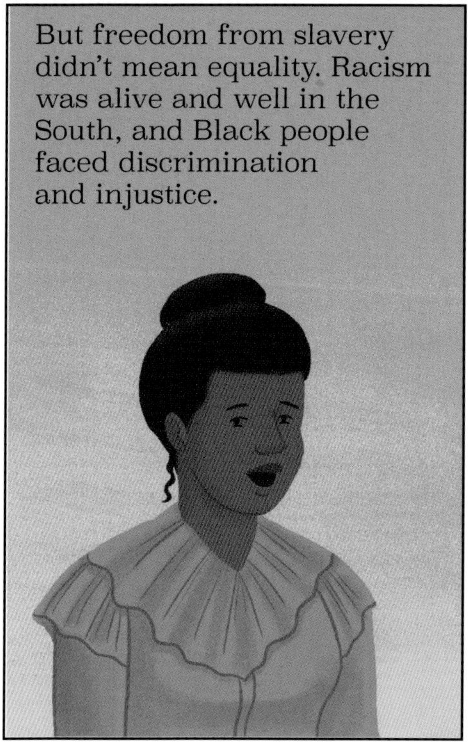
But freedom from slavery didn't mean equality. Racism was alive and well in the South, and Black people faced discrimination and injustice.

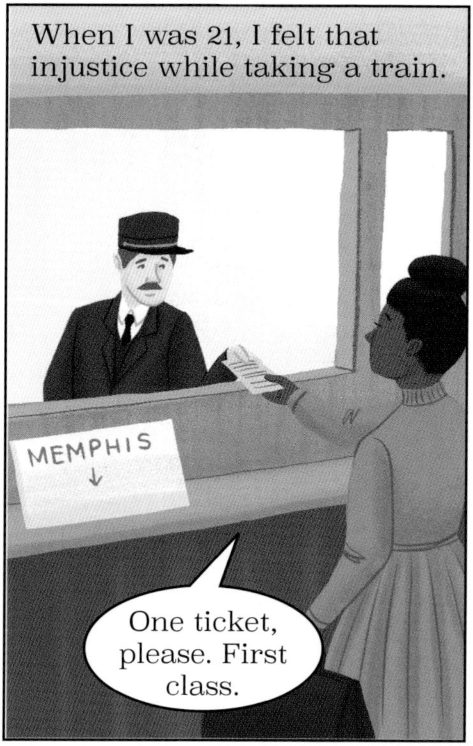
When I was 21, I felt that injustice while taking a train.
MEMPHIS
One ticket, please. First class.

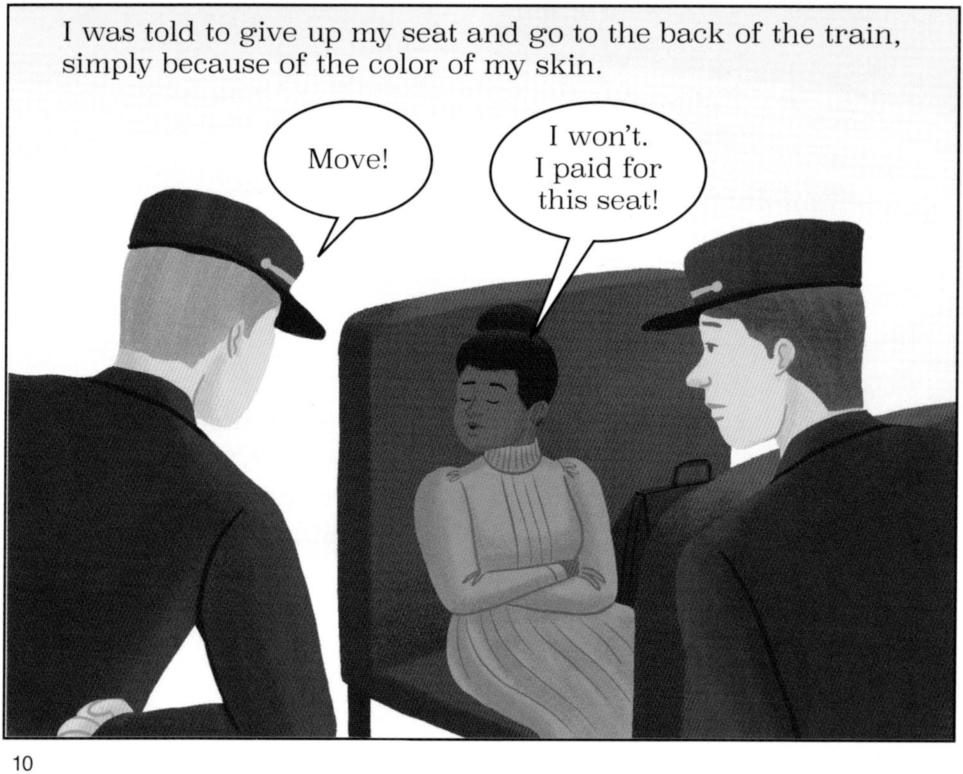
I was told to give up my seat and go to the back of the train, simply because of the color of my skin.
Move!
I won't. I paid for this seat!

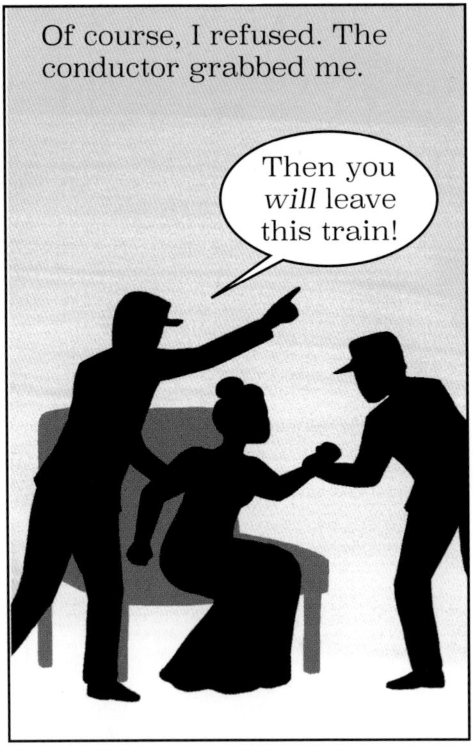
Of course, I refused. The conductor grabbed me.
Then you *will* leave this train!

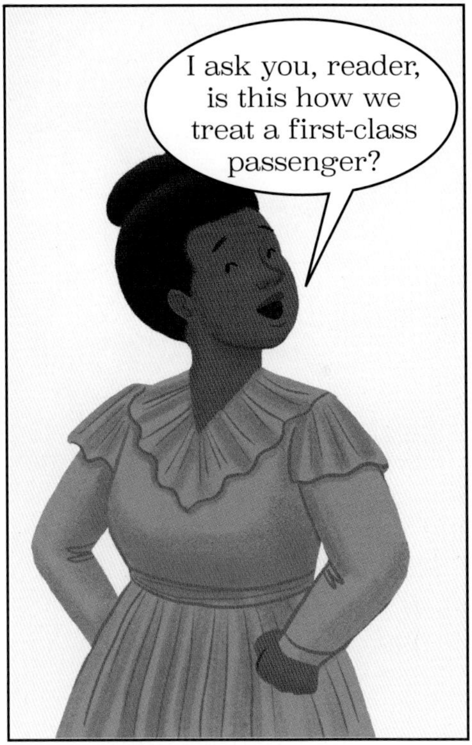
I ask you, reader, is this how we treat a first-class passenger?

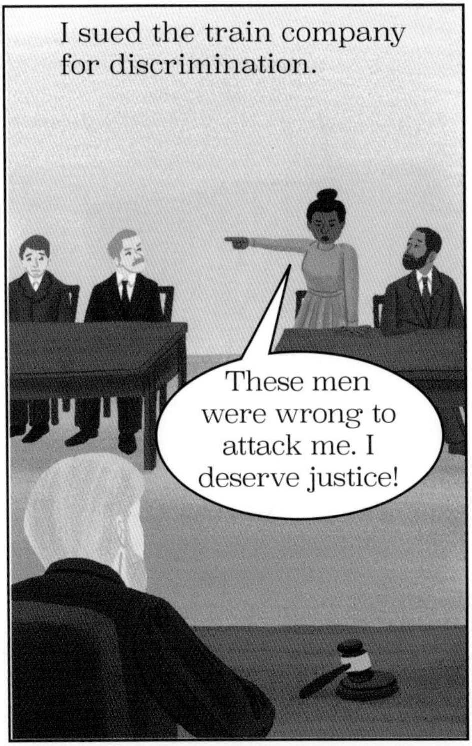
I sued the train company for discrimination.
These men were wrong to attack me. I deserve justice!

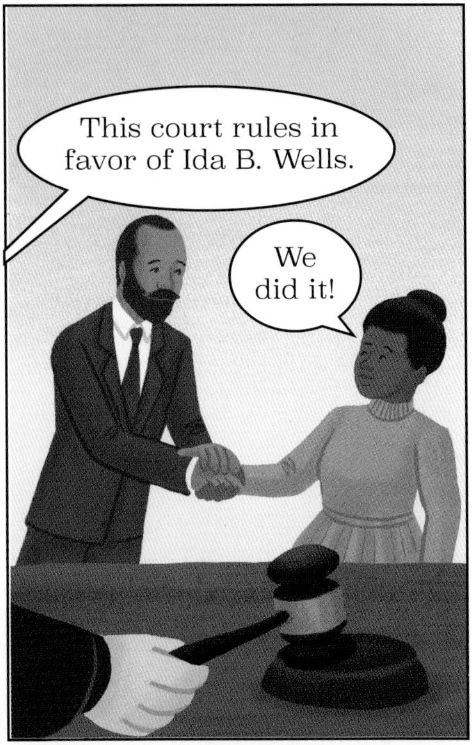
This court rules in favor of Ida B. Wells.
We did it!

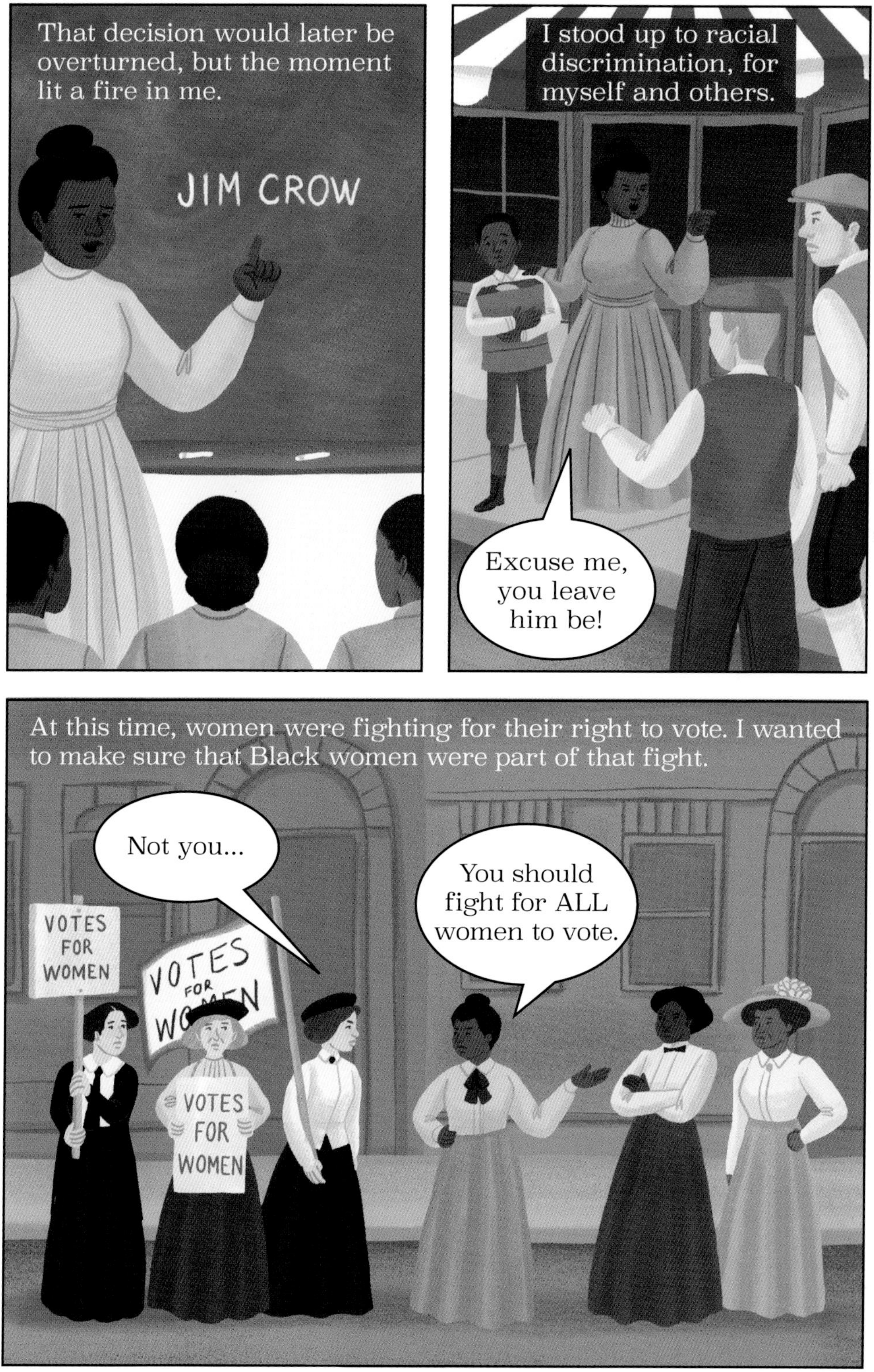
That decision would later be overturned, but the moment lit a fire in me.
JIM CROW
I stood up to racial discrimination, for myself and others.
Excuse me, you leave him be!
At this time, women were fighting for their right to vote. I wanted to make sure that Black women were part of that fight.
VOTES FOR WOMEN
VOTES FOR WOMEN
Not you...
VOTES FOR WOMEN
You should fight for ALL women to vote.

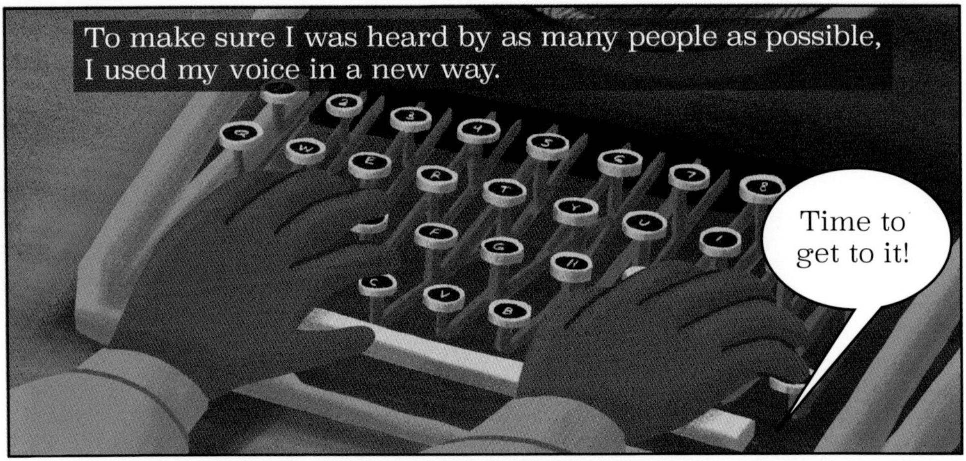
To make sure I was heard by as many people as possible, I used my voice in a new way.
Time to get to it!

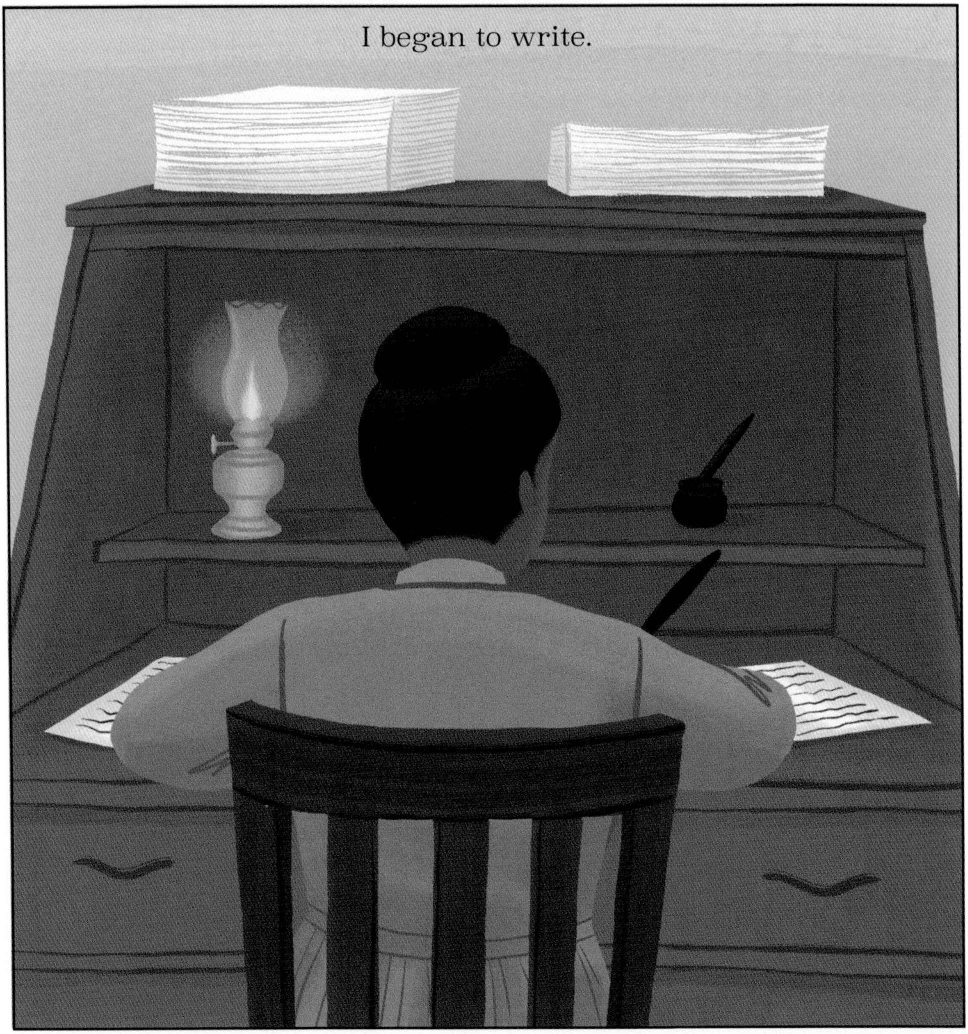
I began to write.

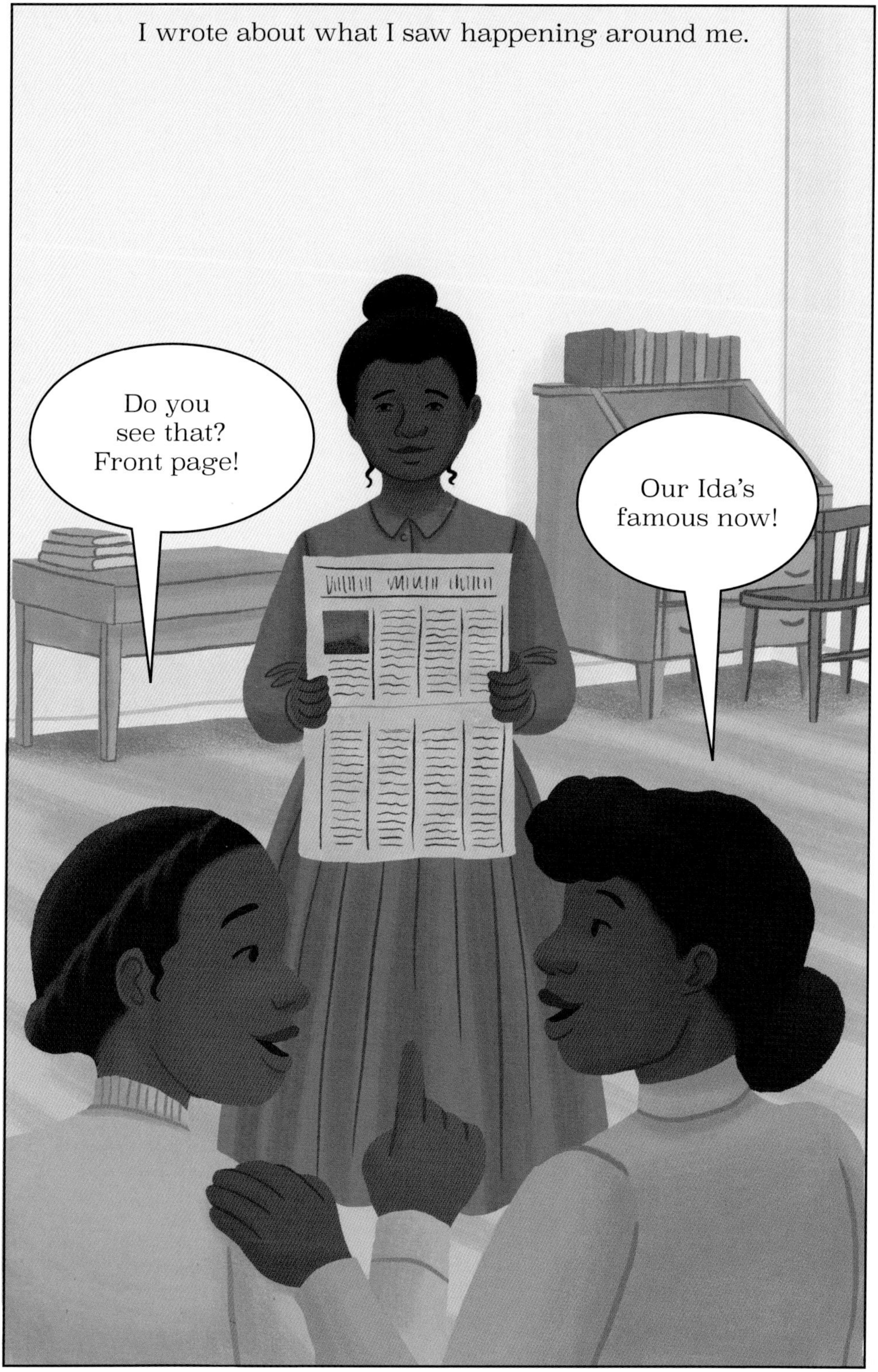
I wrote about what I saw happening around me.
Do you see that? Front page!
Our Ida's famous now!

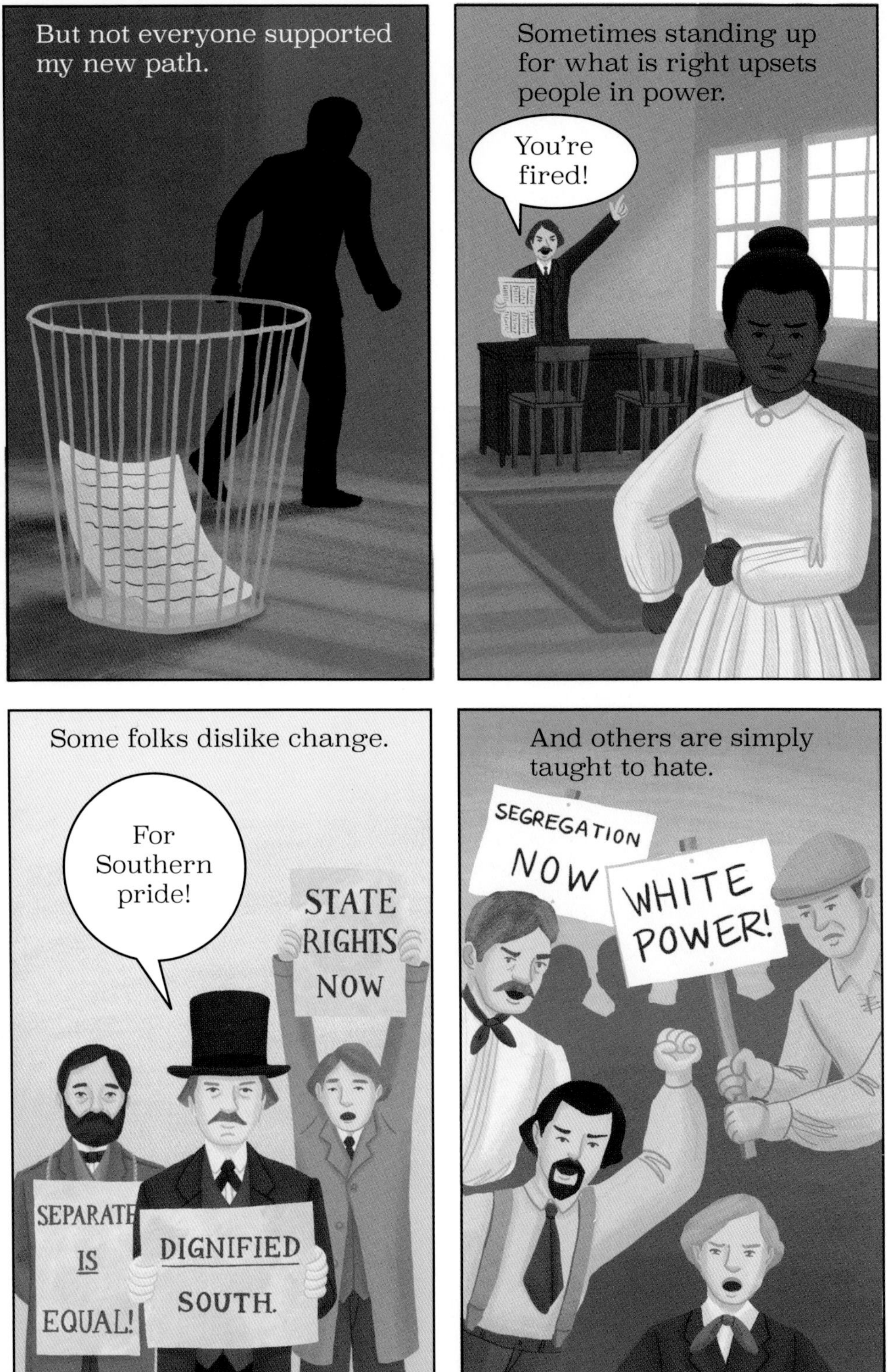
But not everyone supported my new path.
Sometimes standing up for what is right upsets people in power.
You're fired!
Some folks dislike change.
For Southern pride!
STATE RIGHTS NOW
SEPARATE IS EQUAL!
DIGNIFIED SOUTH.
And others are simply taught to hate.
SEGREGATION NOW
WHITE POWER!

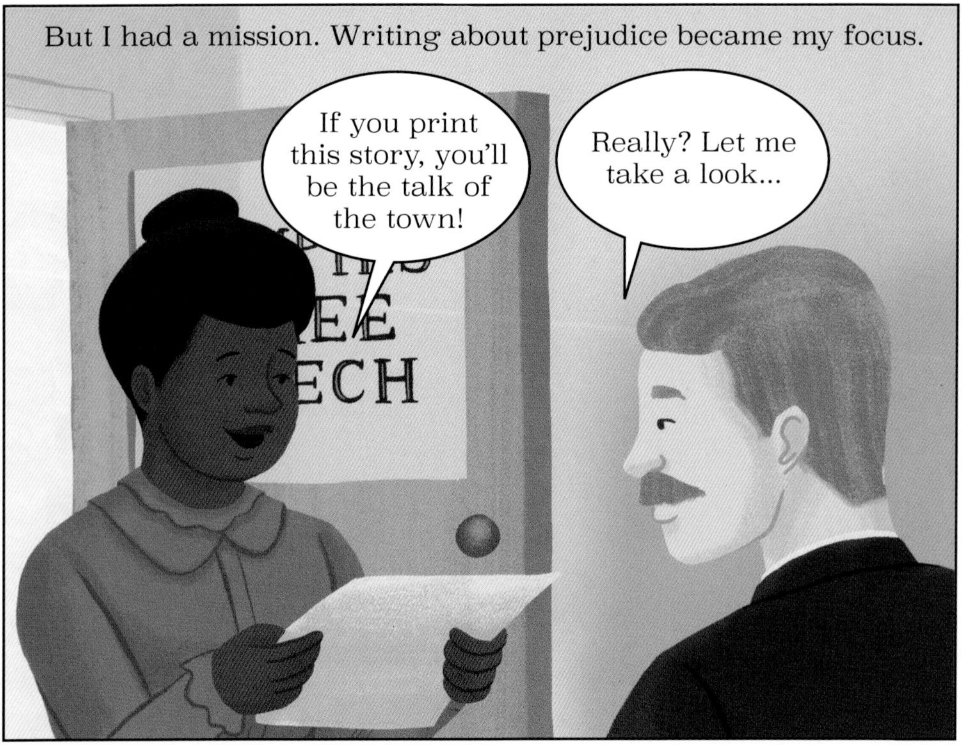
But I had a mission. Writing about prejudice became my focus.
If you print this story, you'll be the talk of the town!
Really? Let me take a look...

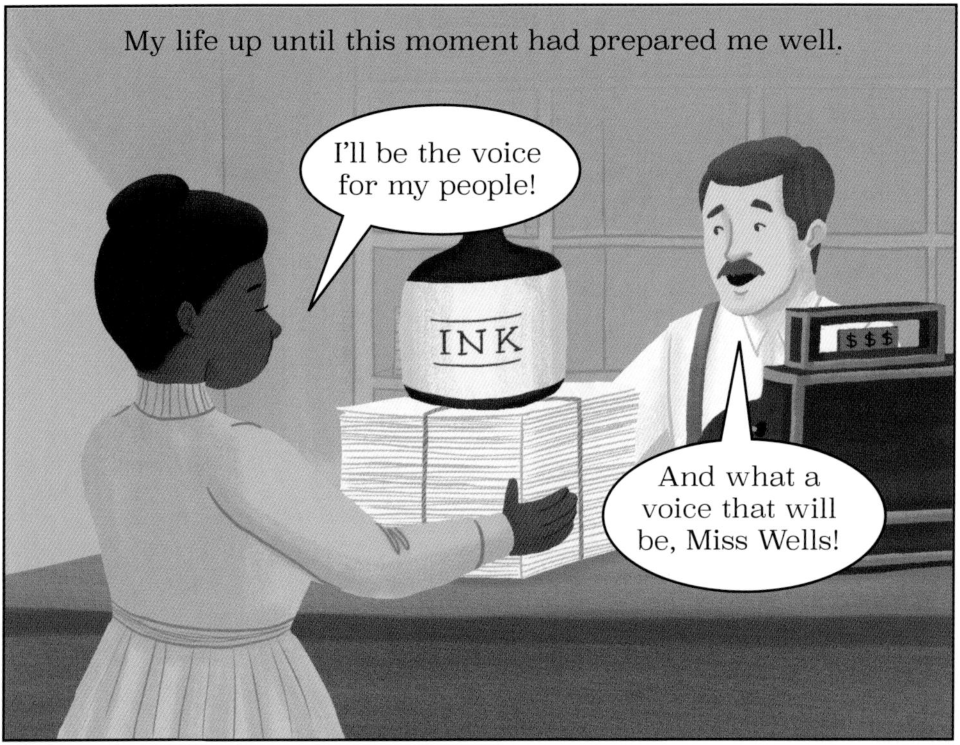
My life up until this moment had prepared me well.
I'll be the voice for my people!
INK
And what a voice that will be, Miss Wells!

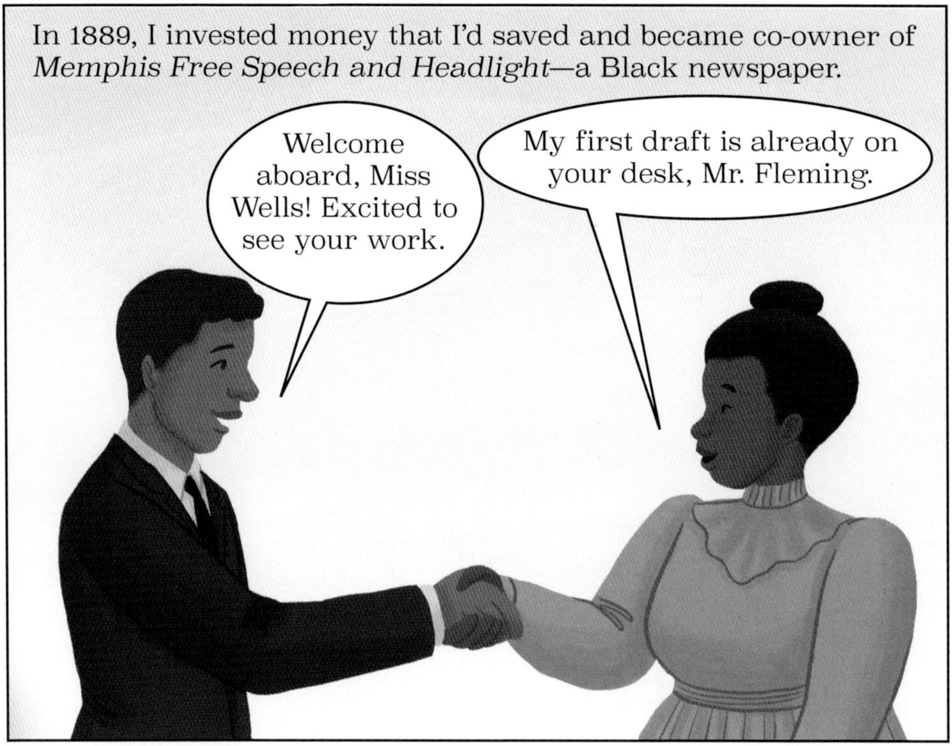
In 1889, I invested money that I'd saved and became co-owner of *Memphis Free Speech and Headlight*—a Black newspaper.
Welcome aboard, Miss Wells! Excited to see your work.
My first draft is already on your desk, Mr. Fleming.

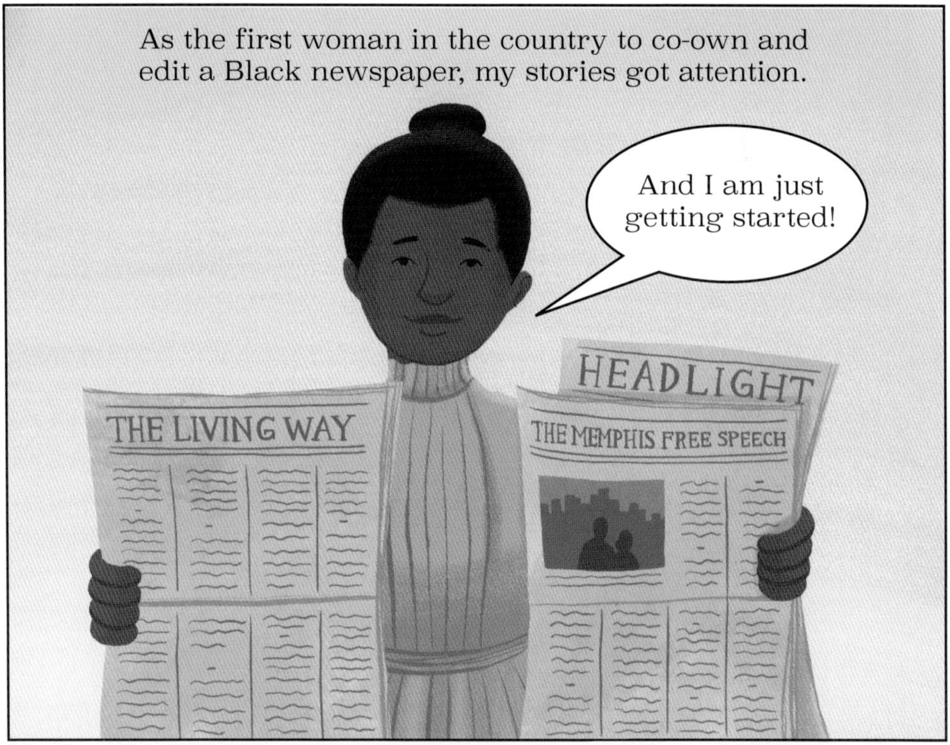
As the first woman in the country to co-own and edit a Black newspaper, my stories got attention.
And I am just getting started!
HEADLIGHT
THE LIVING WAY
THE MEMPHIS FREE SPEECH

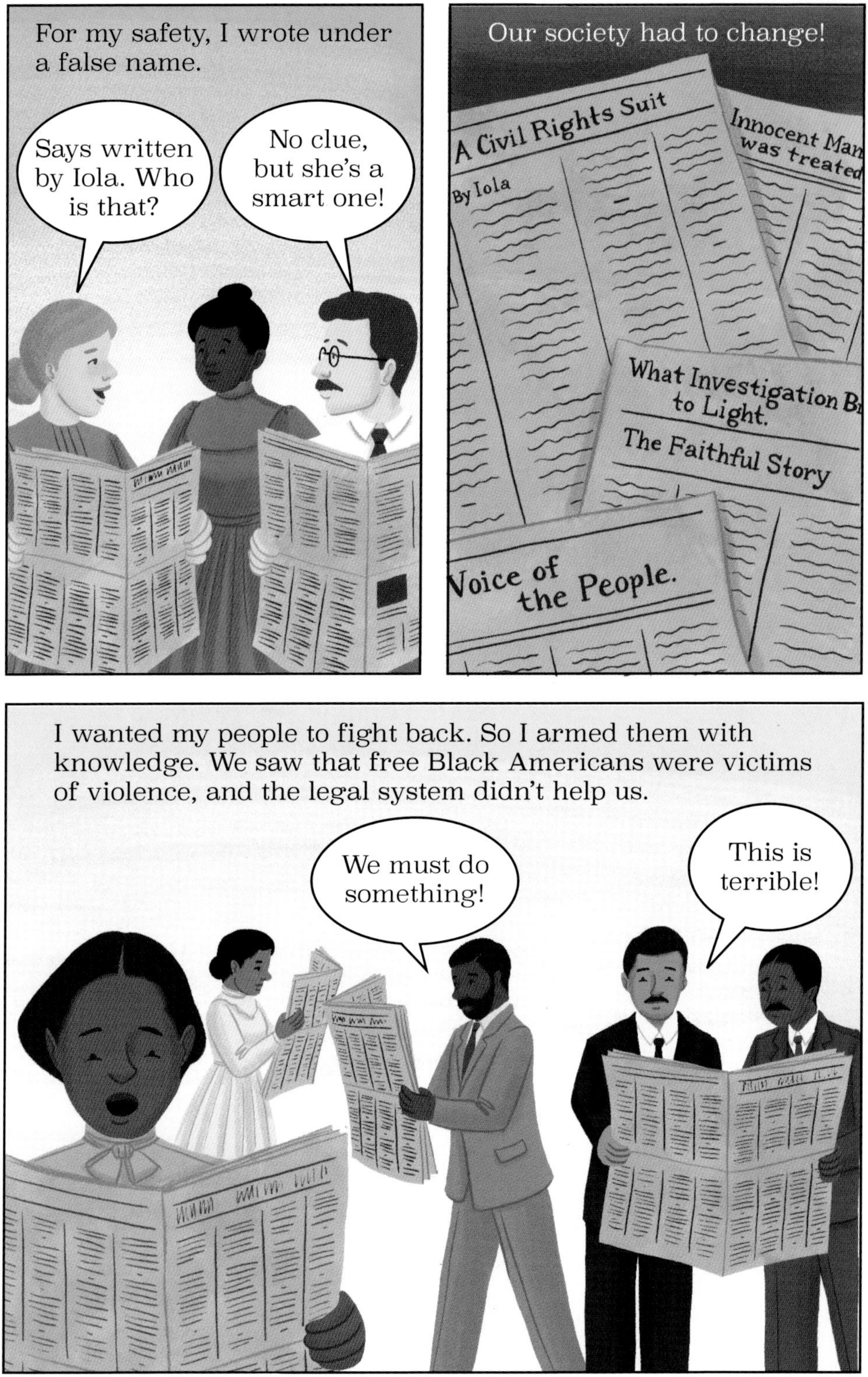
For my safety, I wrote under a false name.
Says written by Iola. Who is that?
No clue, but she's a smart one!
Our society had to change!
A Civil Rights Suit
By Iola
Innocent Man was treated
What Investigation Br to Light.
The Faithful Story
Voice of the People.
I wanted my people to fight back. So I armed them with knowledge. We saw that free Black Americans were victims of violence, and the legal system didn't help us.
We must do something!
This is terrible!

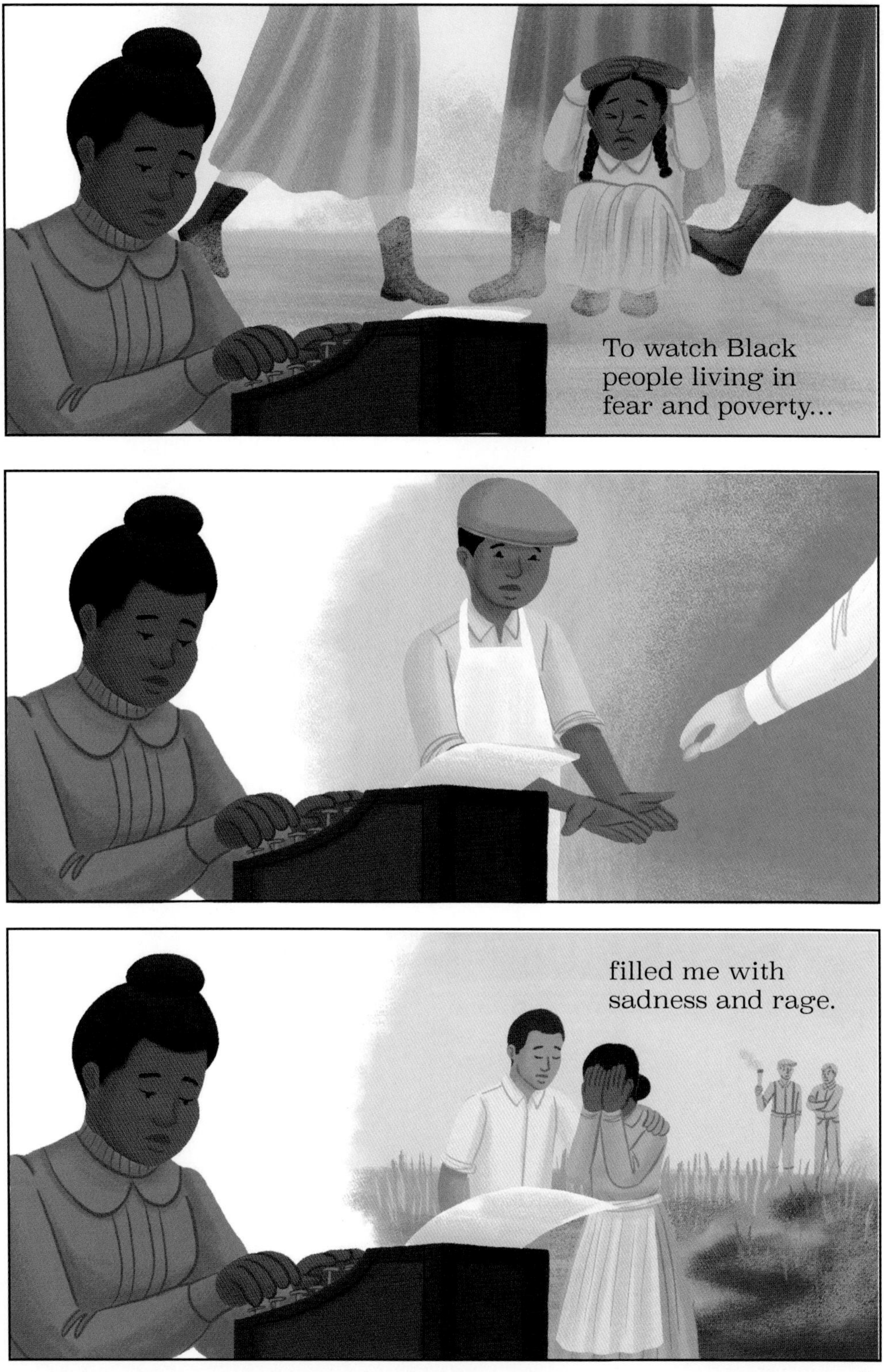
To watch Black people living in fear and poverty...
filled me with sadness and rage.

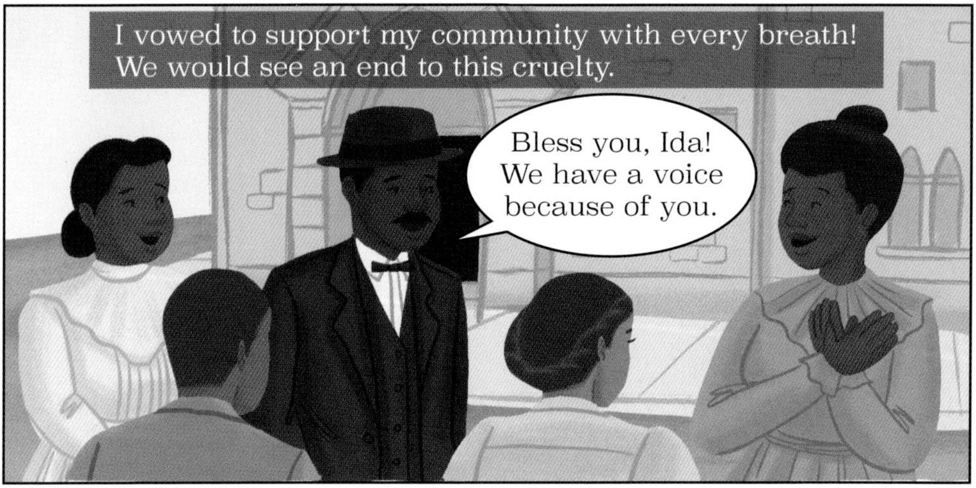
I vowed to support my community with every breath! We would see an end to this cruelty.
Bless you, Ida! We have a voice because of you.

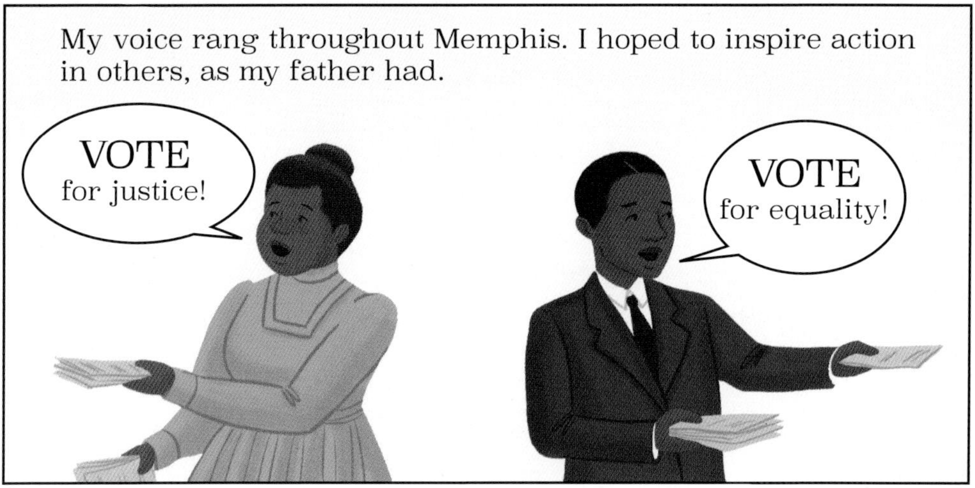
My voice rang throughout Memphis. I hoped to inspire action in others, as my father had.
VOTE for justice!
VOTE for equality!

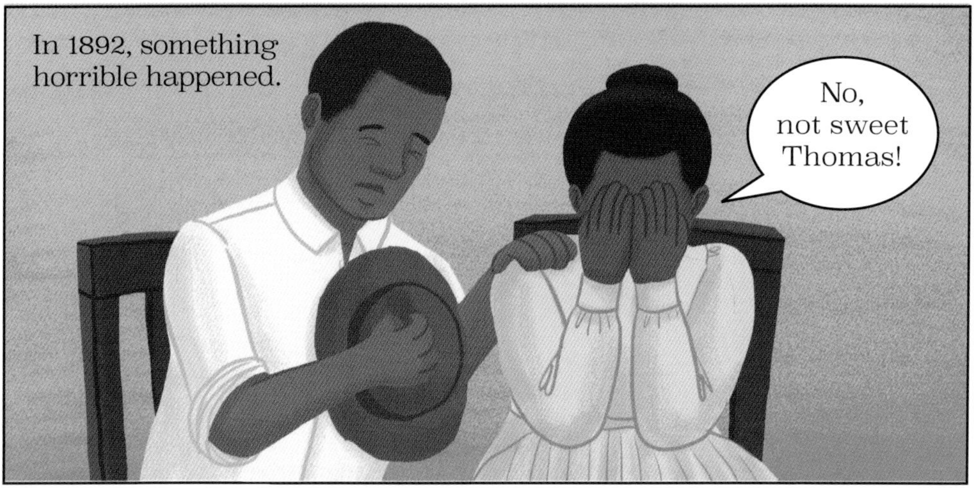
In 1892, something horrible happened.
No, not sweet Thomas!

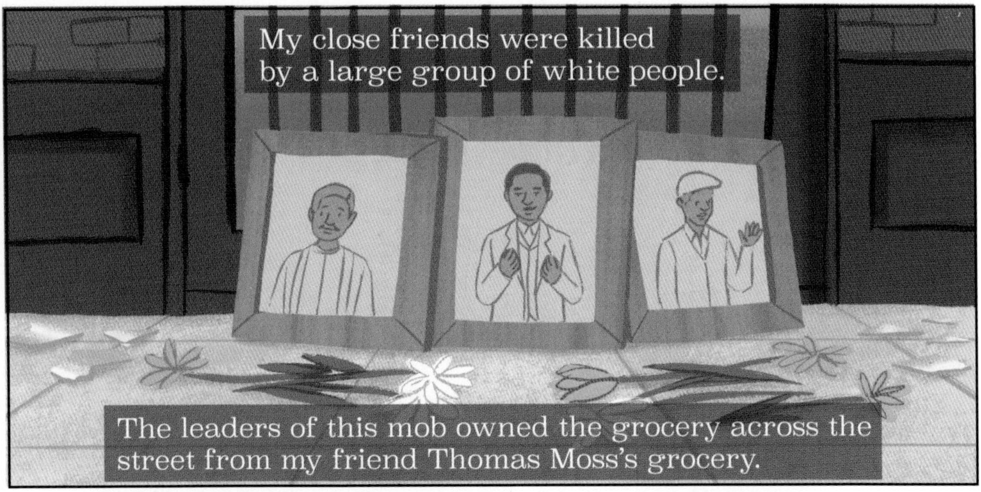
My close friends were killed by a large group of white people.
The leaders of this mob owned the grocery across the street from my friend Thomas Moss's grocery.

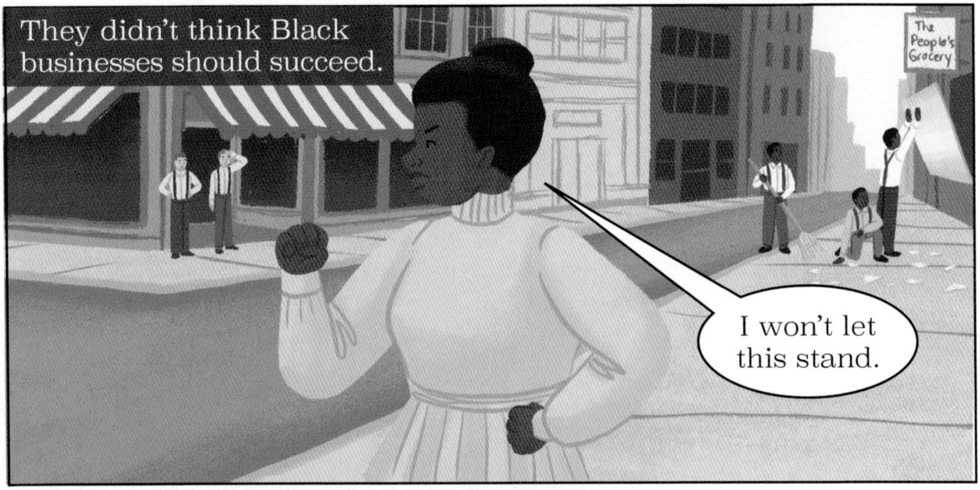
They didn't think Black businesses should succeed.
The People's Grocery
I won't let this stand.

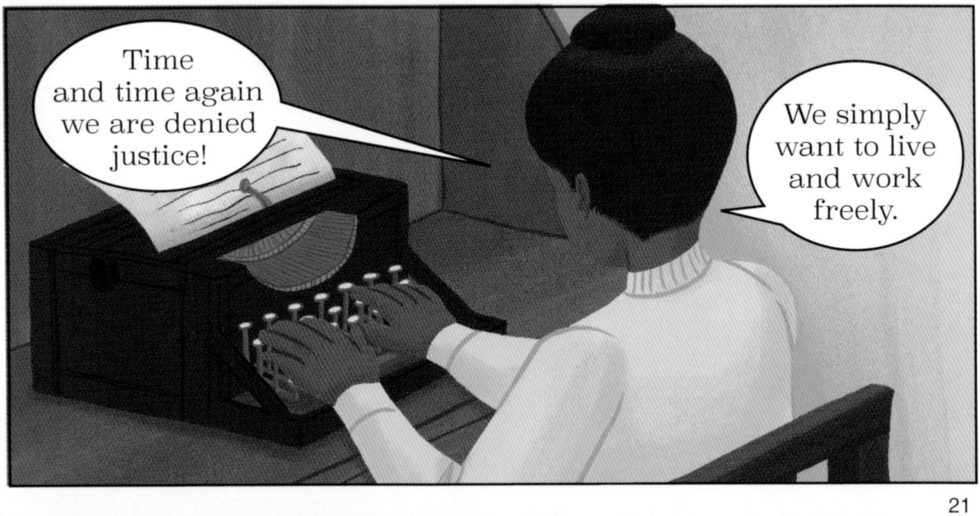
Time and time again we are denied justice!
We simply want to live and work freely.

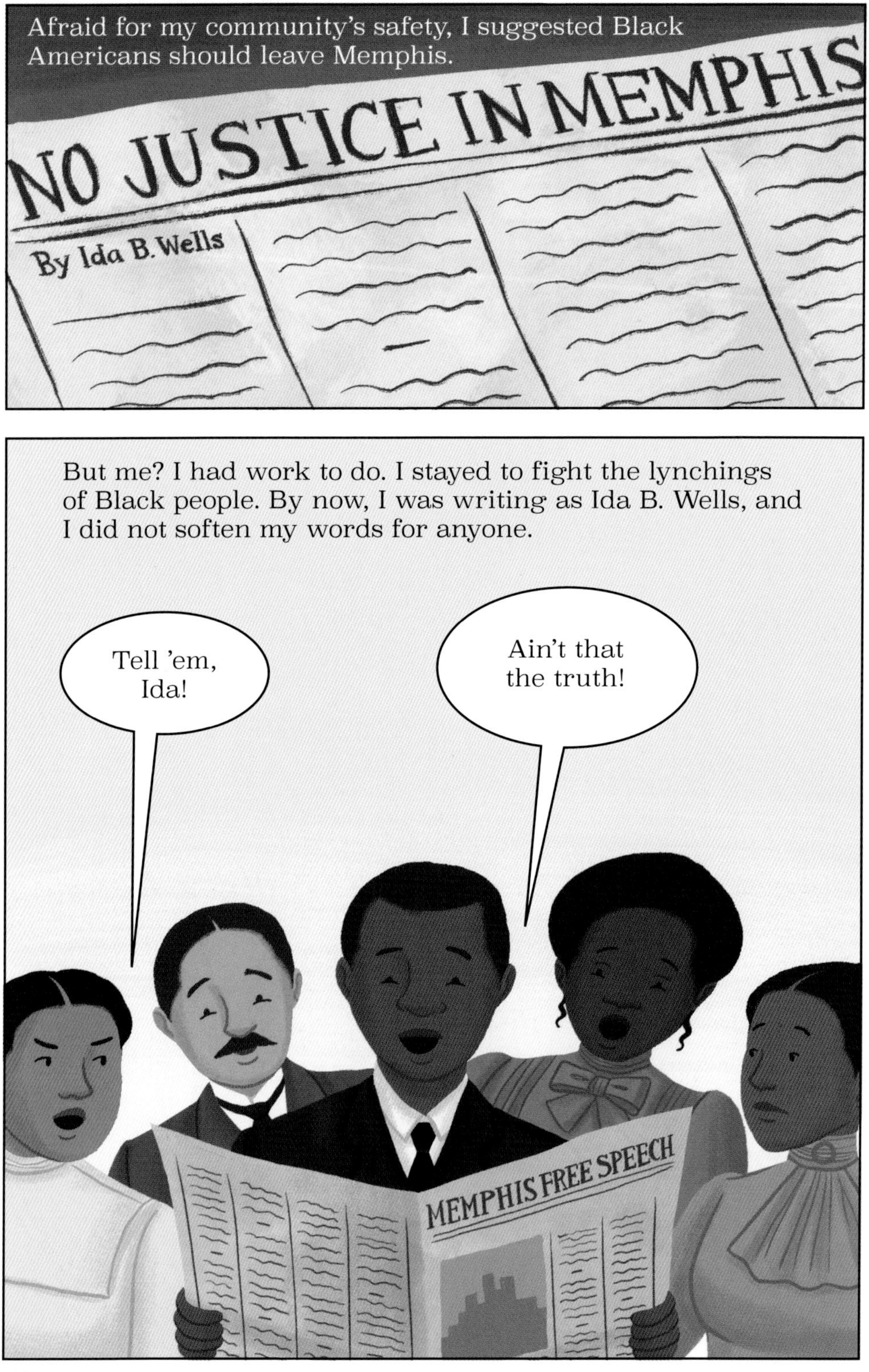
Afraid for my community's safety, I suggested Black Americans should leave Memphis.
NO JUSTICE IN MEMPHIS
By Ida B. Wells
But me? I had work to do. I stayed to fight the lynchings of Black people. By now, I was writing as Ida B. Wells, and I did not soften my words for anyone.
Tell 'em, Ida!
Ain't that the truth!
MEMPHIS FREE SPEECH

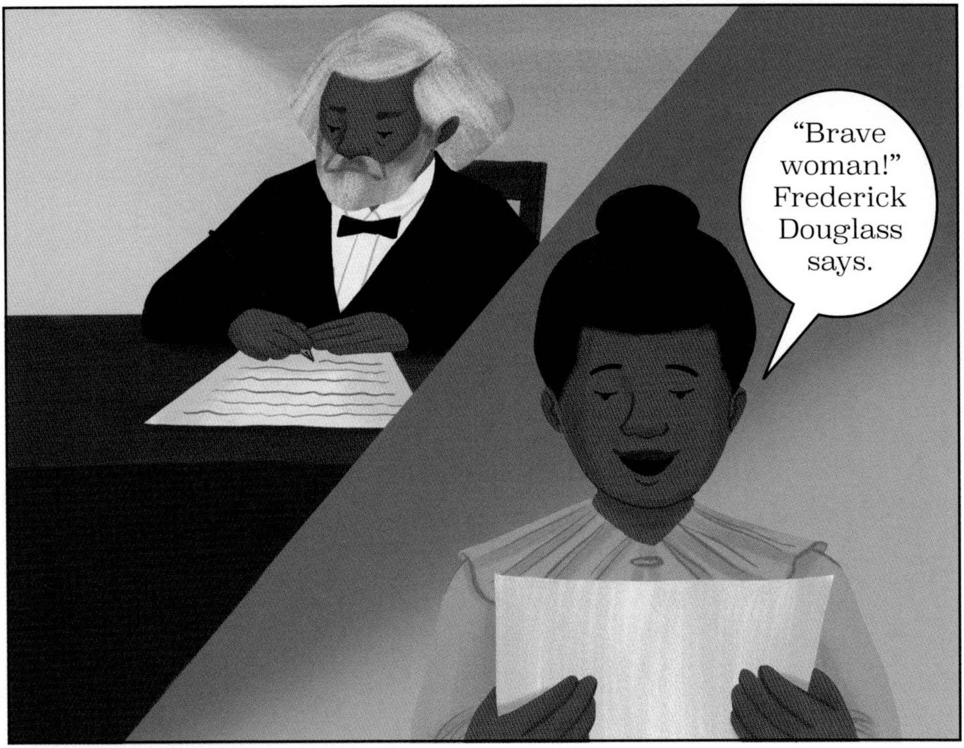
"Brave woman!" Frederick Douglass says.

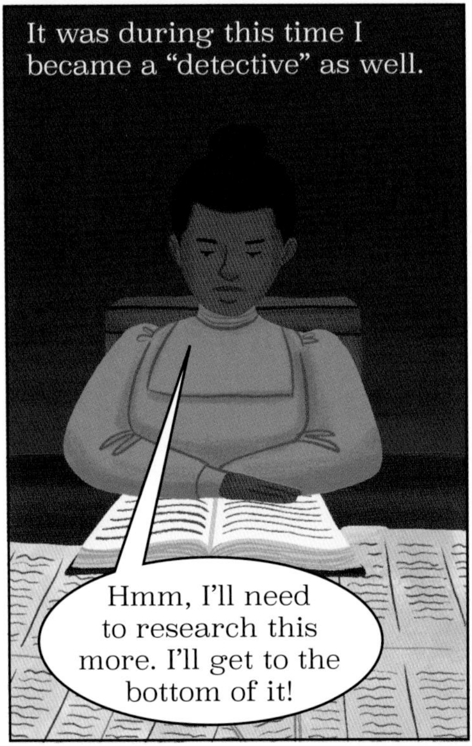
It was during this time I became a "detective" as well.
Hmm, I'll need to research this more. I'll get to the bottom of it!

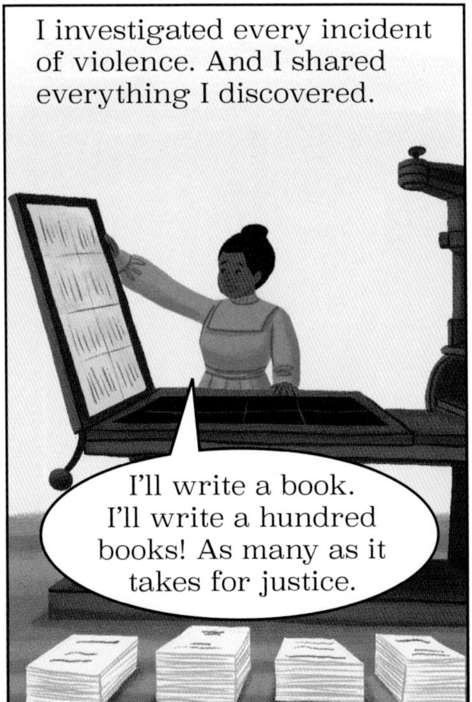
I investigated every incident of violence. And I shared everything I discovered.
I'll write a book. I'll write a hundred books! As many as it takes for justice.

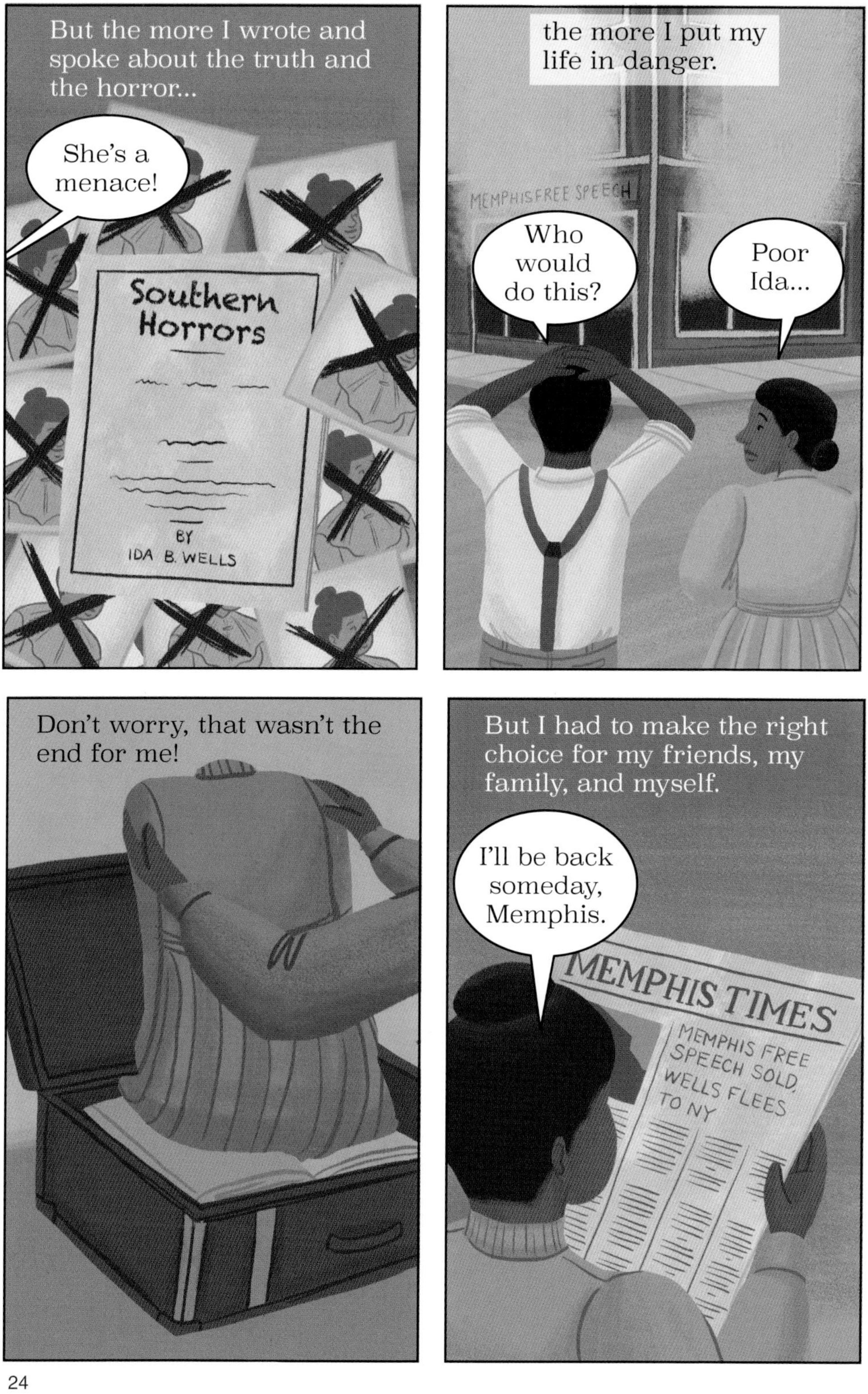
But the more I wrote and spoke about the truth and the horror...
She's a menace!
Southern Horrors
BY
IDA B. WELLS
the more I put my life in danger.
MEMPHIS FREE SPEECH
Who would do this?
Poor Ida...
Don't worry, that wasn't the end for me!
But I had to make the right choice for my friends, my family, and myself.
I'll be back someday, Memphis.
MEMPHIS TIMES
MEMPHIS FREE SPEECH SOLD, WELLS FLEES TO NY

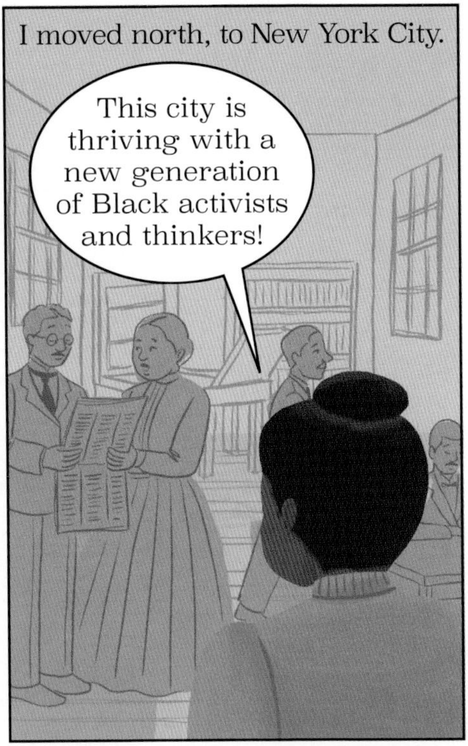
I moved north, to New York City.
This city is thriving with a new generation of Black activists and thinkers!

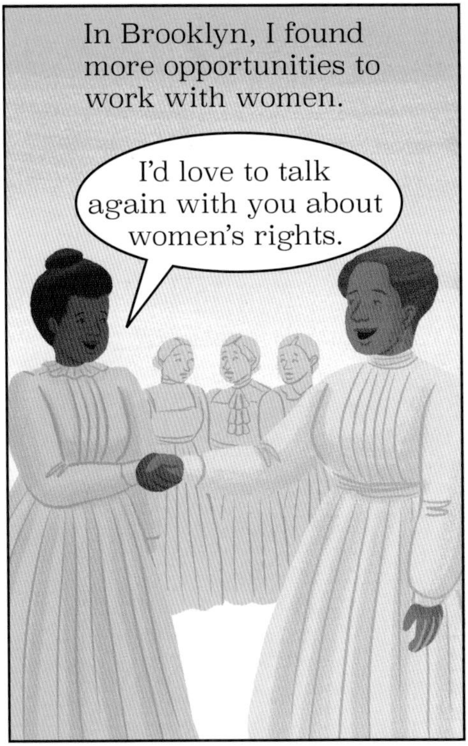
In Brooklyn, I found more opportunities to work with women.
I'd love to talk again with you about women's rights.

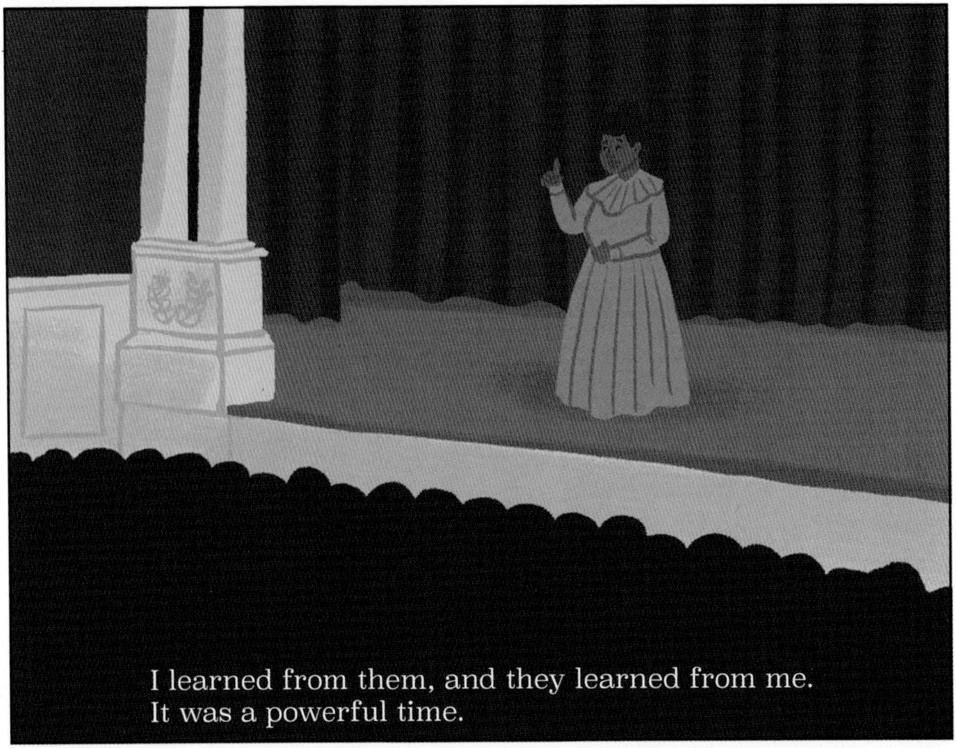
I learned from them, and they learned from me.
It was a powerful time.

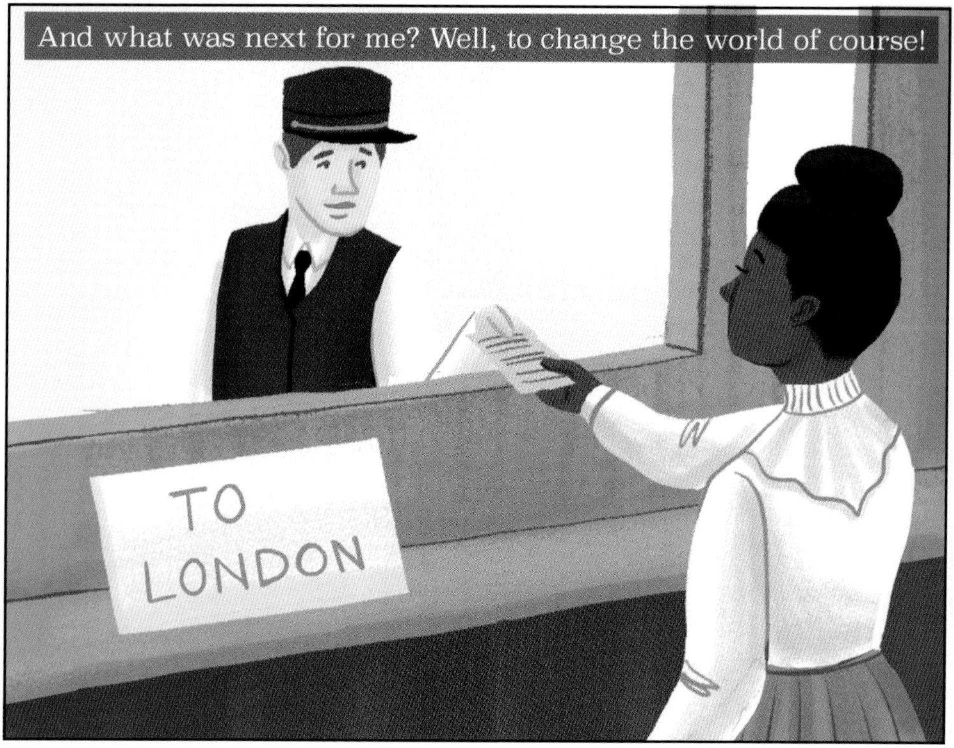
And what was next for me? Well, to change the world of course!
TO LONDON

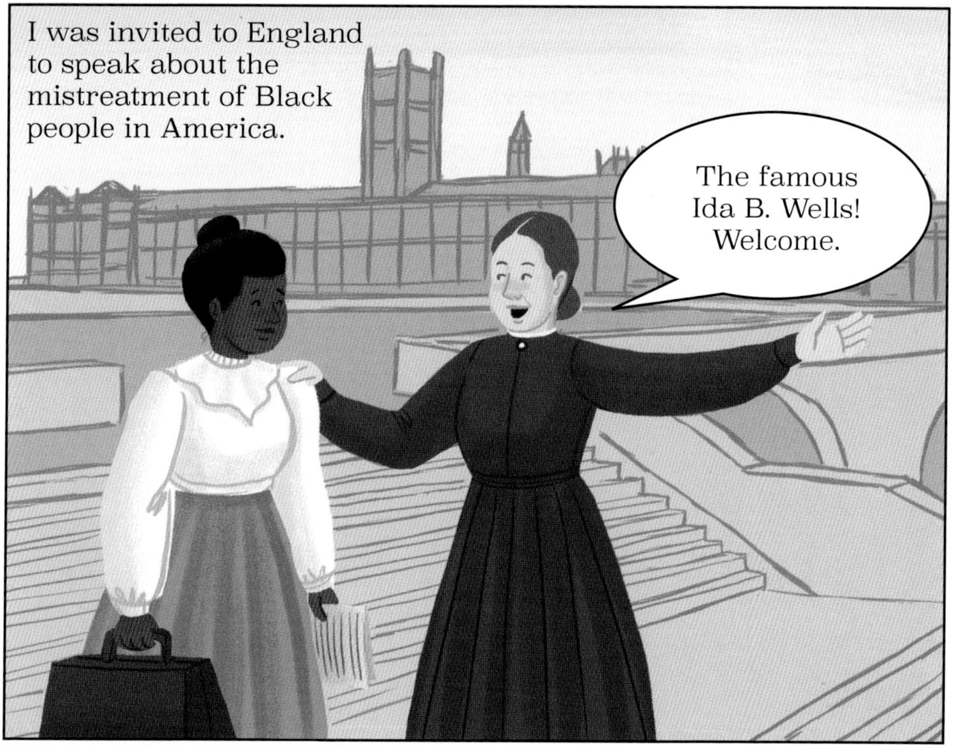
I was invited to England to speak about the mistreatment of Black people in America.
The famous Ida B. Wells! Welcome.

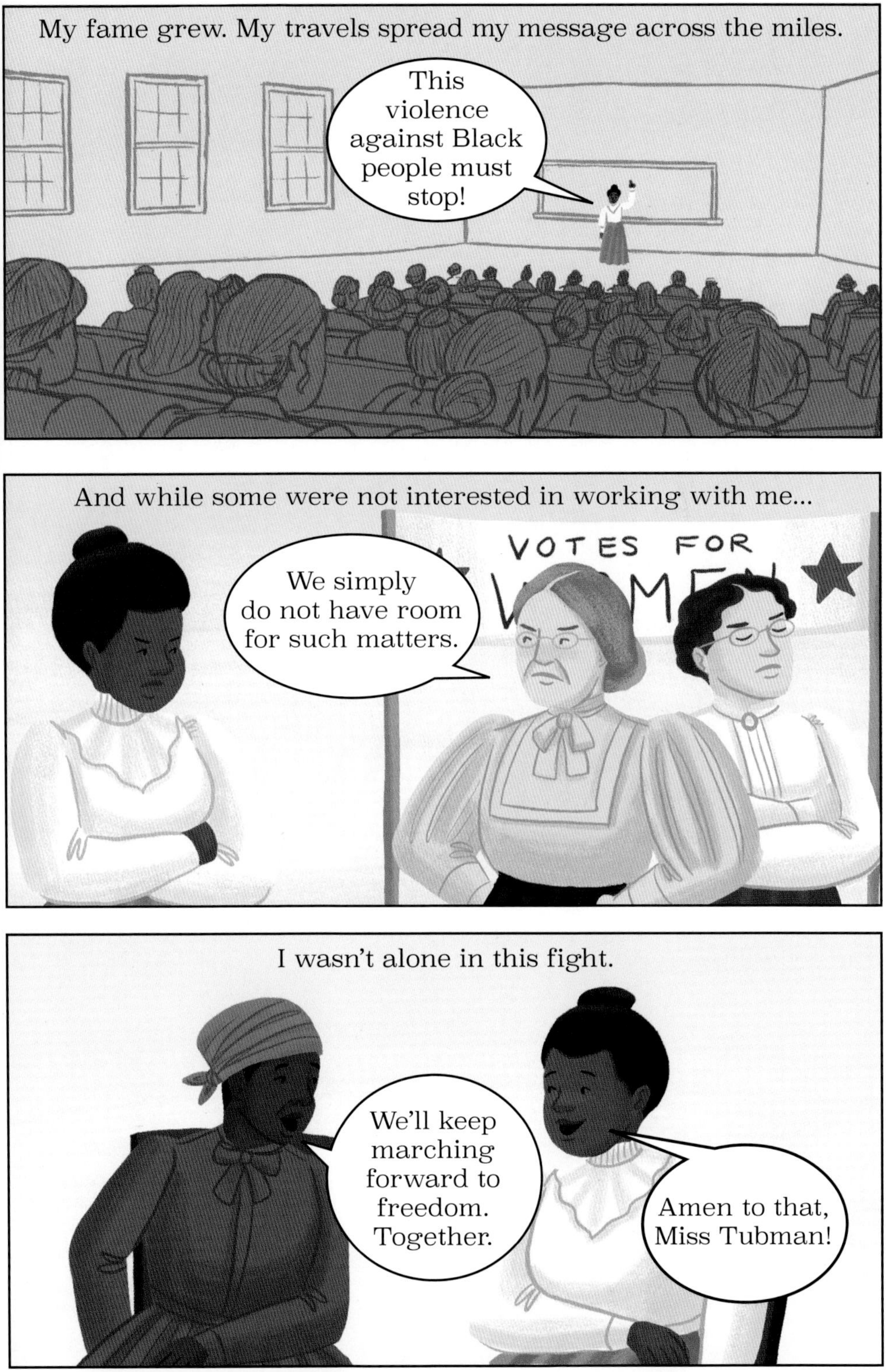
My fame grew. My travels spread my message across the miles.
This violence against Black people must stop!
And while some were not interested in working with me...
VOTES FOR
We simply do not have room for such matters.
I wasn't alone in this fight.
We'll keep marching forward to freedom. Together.
Amen to that, Miss Tubman!

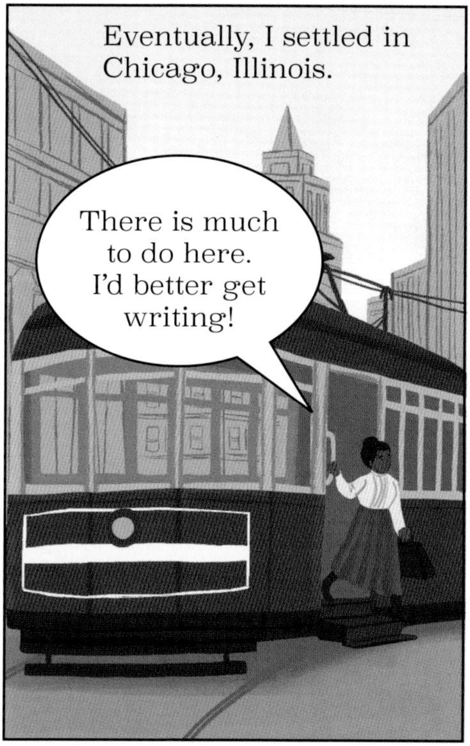
Eventually, I settled in Chicago, Illinois.
There is much to do here. I'd better get writing!

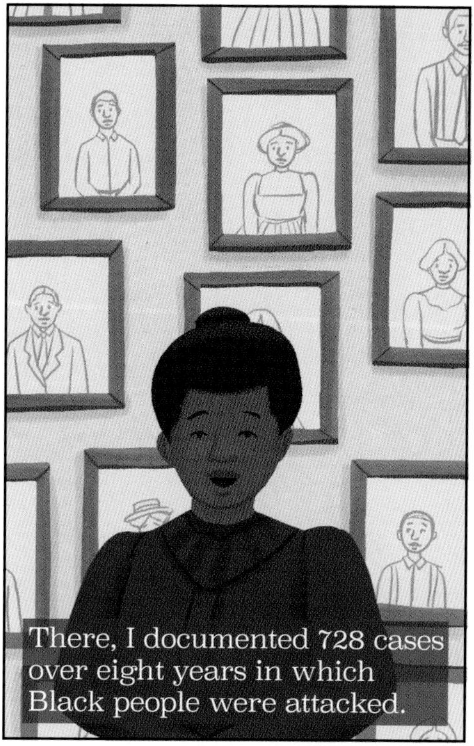
There, I documented 728 cases over eight years in which Black people were attacked.

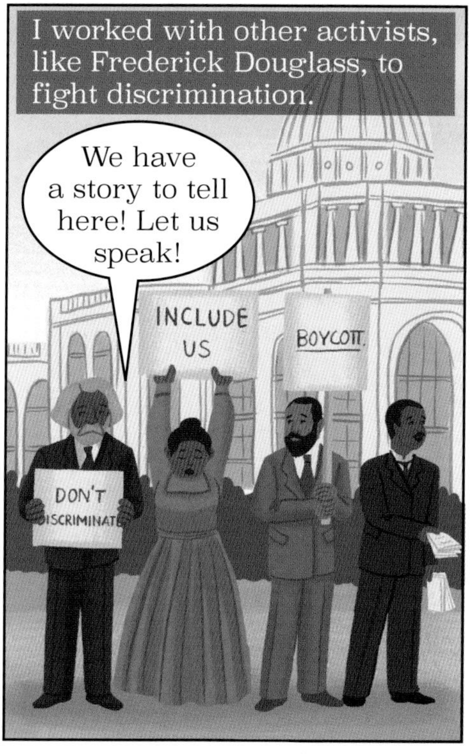
I worked with other activists, like Frederick Douglass, to fight discrimination.
We have a story to tell here! Let us speak!
INCLUDE US
BOYCOTT
DON'T ISCRIMINAT

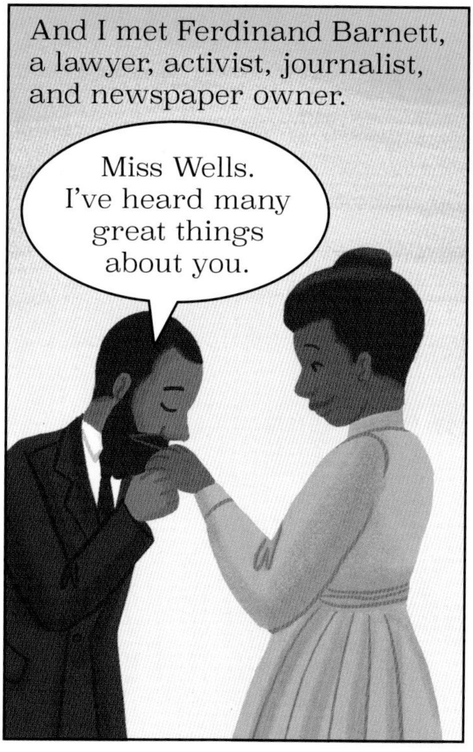
And I met Ferdinand Barnett, a lawyer, activist, journalist, and newspaper owner.
Miss Wells. I've heard many great things about you.

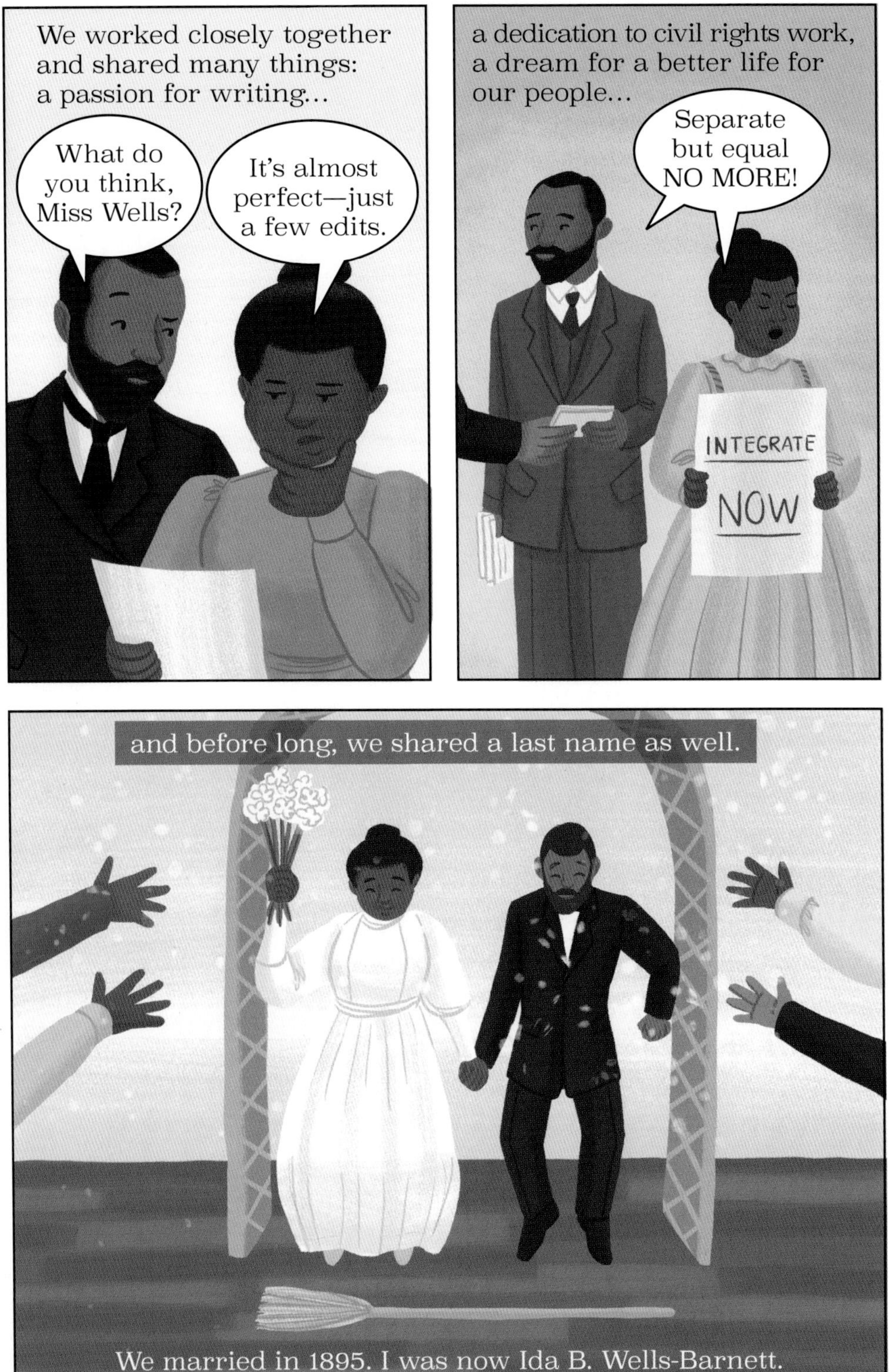

We worked closely together and shared many things: a passion for writing...
What do you think, Miss Wells?
It's almost perfect—just a few edits.
a dedication to civil rights work, a dream for a better life for our people...
Separate but equal NO MORE!
INTEGRATE NOW
and before long, we shared a last name as well.
We married in 1895. I was now Ida B. Wells-Barnett.

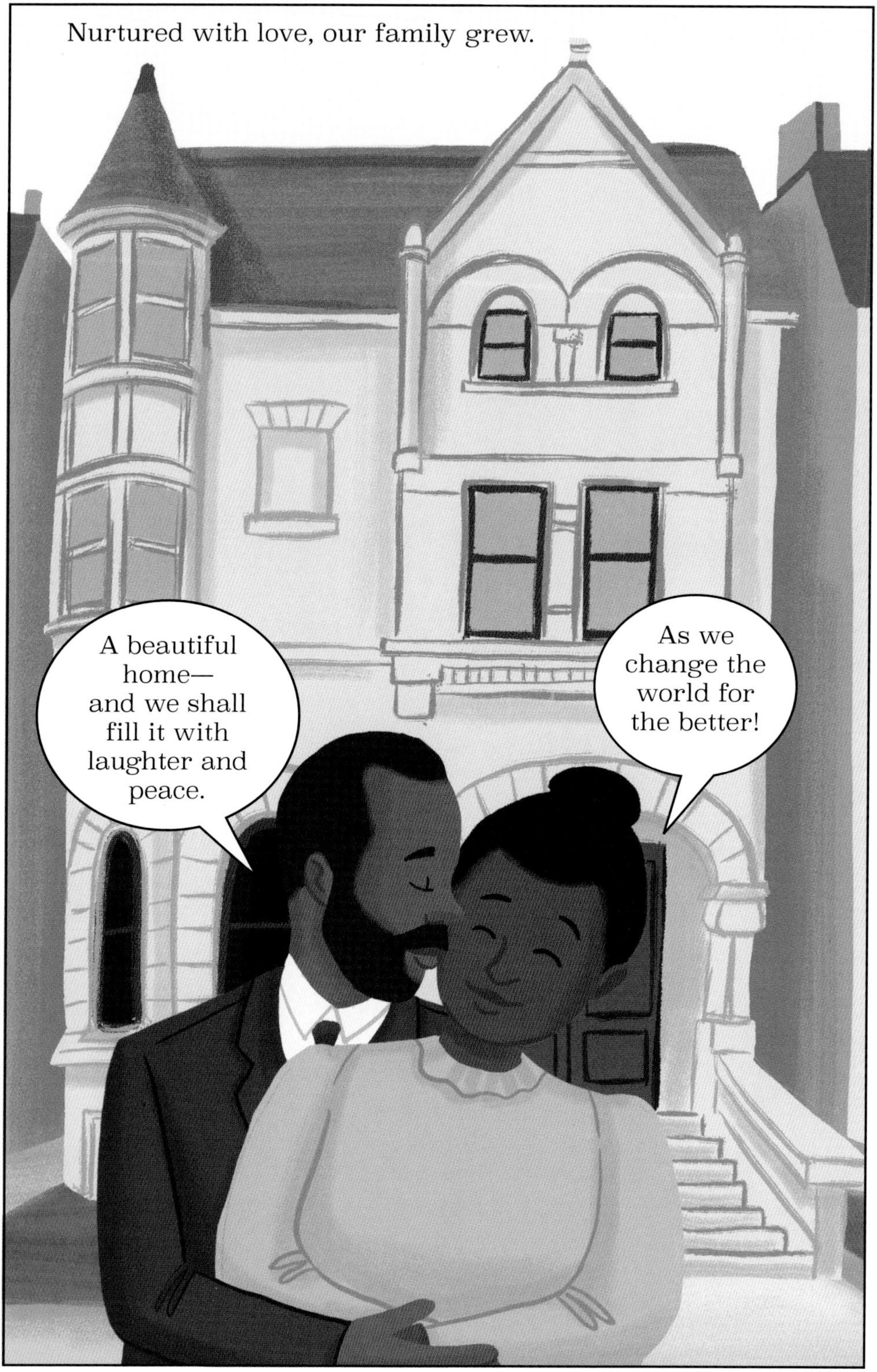
Nurtured with love, our family grew.
A beautiful home—and we shall fill it with laughter and peace.
As we change the world for the better!

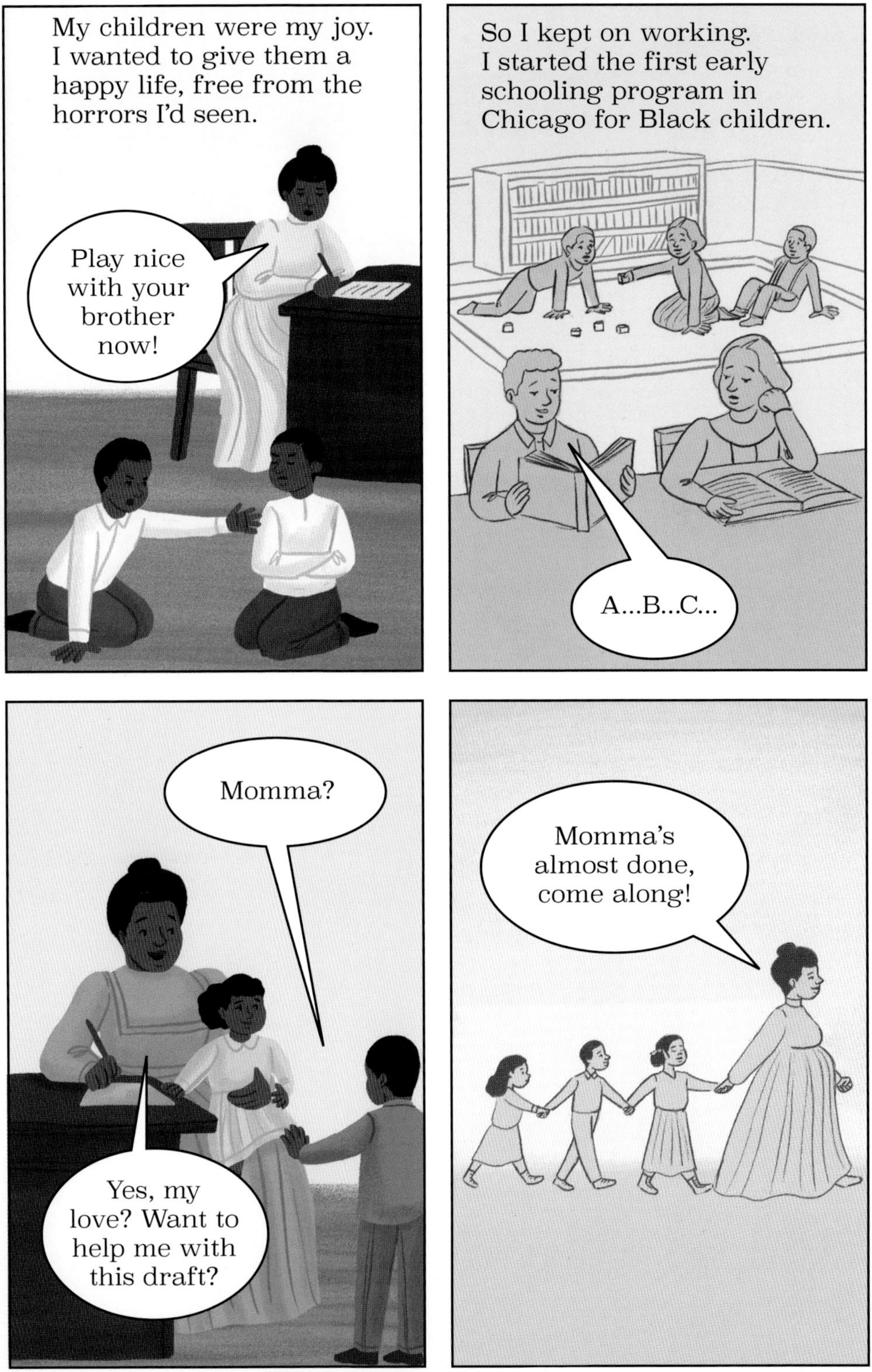
My children were my joy. I wanted to give them a happy life, free from the horrors I'd seen.
Play nice with your brother now!
So I kept on working. I started the first early schooling program in Chicago for Black children.
A...B...C...
Momma?
Yes, my love? Want to help me with this draft?
Momma's almost done, come along!

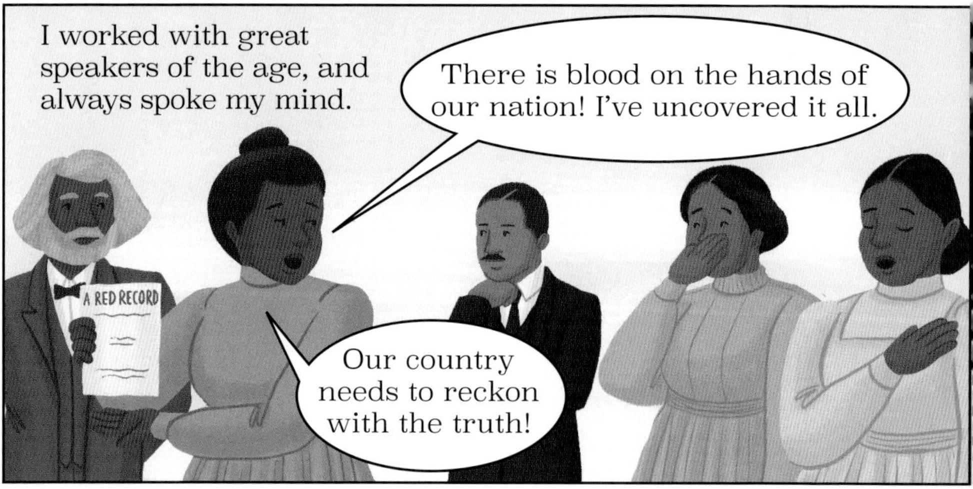
I worked with great speakers of the age, and always spoke my mind.
There is blood on the hands of our nation! I've uncovered it all.
A RED RECORD
Our country needs to reckon with the truth!

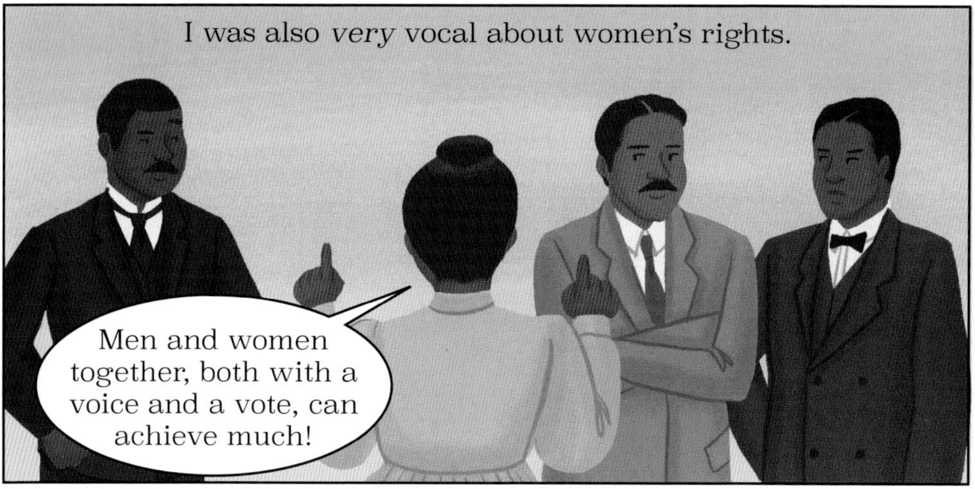
I was also *very* vocal about women's rights.
Men and women together, both with a voice and a vote, can achieve much!

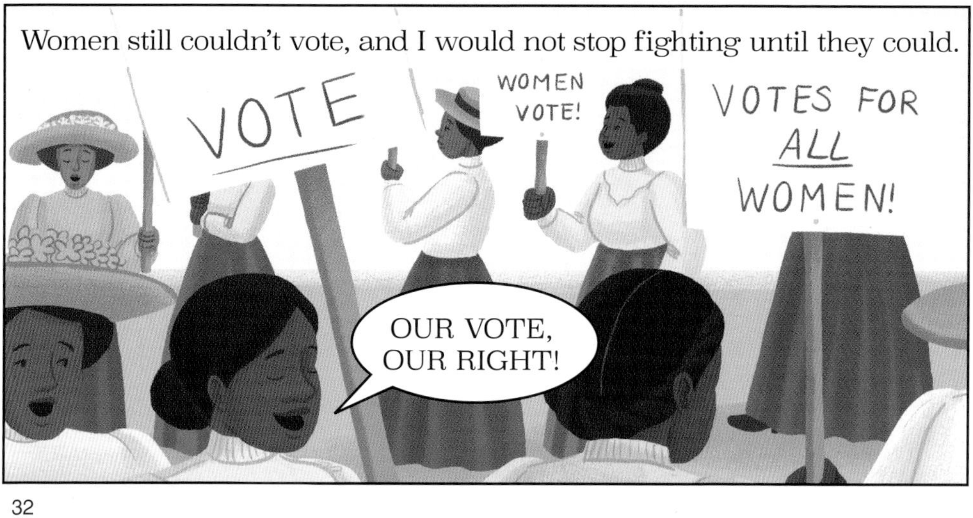
Women still couldn't vote, and I would not stop fighting until they could.
VOTE
WOMEN VOTE!
VOTES FOR ALL WOMEN!
OUR VOTE, OUR RIGHT!

I wasn't always welcome in women's rights marches, where the leaders were white.

What? We have a right to be here!

But "impossible" was not a word I believed in.

VOTES FOR WOMEN

WOMEN VOTE.

RIGHT TO VOTE

VOTE FOR WOME

VOTE! VOTE!

VOTES FOR WOMEN

WE VOTE

I worked hard. And I deserved a seat at the table.

Pardon me, just finding my spot.

Um...

VOTES

Ahem.

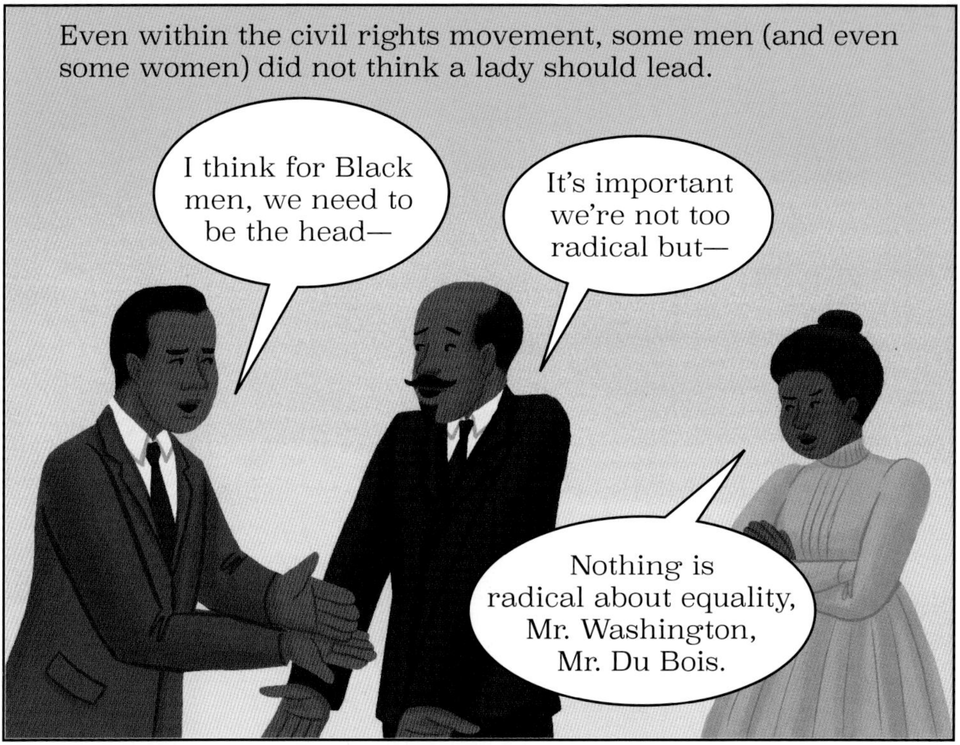
Even within the civil rights movement, some men (and even some women) did not think a lady should lead.
I think for Black men, we need to be the head—
It's important we're not too radical but—
Nothing is radical about equality, Mr. Washington, Mr. Du Bois.

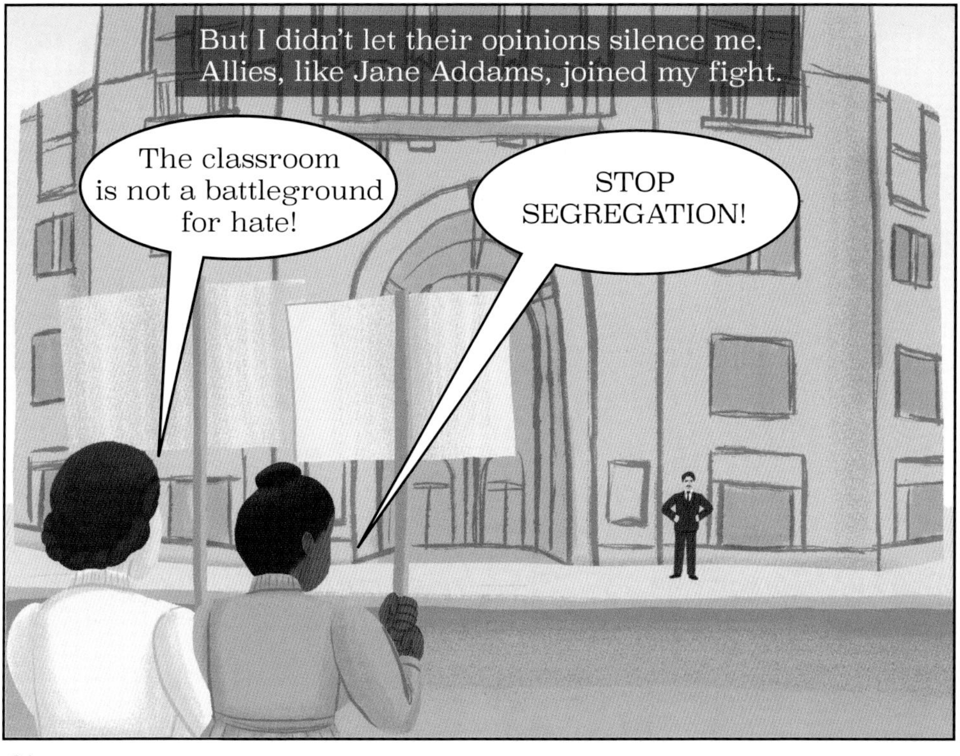
But I didn't let their opinions silence me. Allies, like Jane Addams, joined my fight.
The classroom is not a battleground for hate!
STOP SEGREGATION!

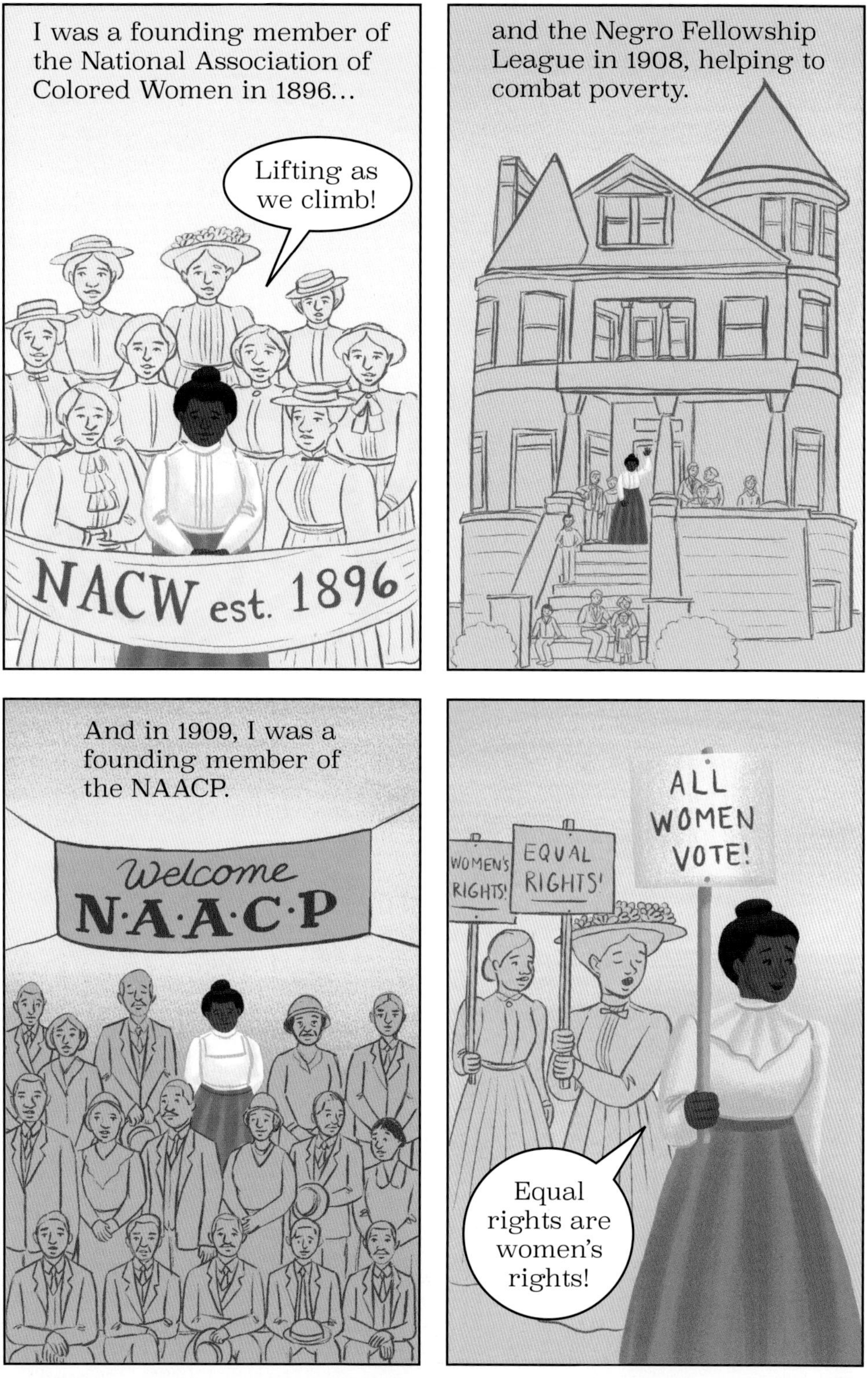
I was a founding member of the National Association of Colored Women in 1896...
Lifting as we climb!
NACW est. 1896
and the Negro Fellowship League in 1908, helping to combat poverty.
And in 1909, I was a founding member of the NAACP.
Welcome N·A·A·C·P
WOMEN'S RIGHTS!
EQUAL RIGHTS!
ALL WOMEN VOTE!
Equal rights are women's rights!

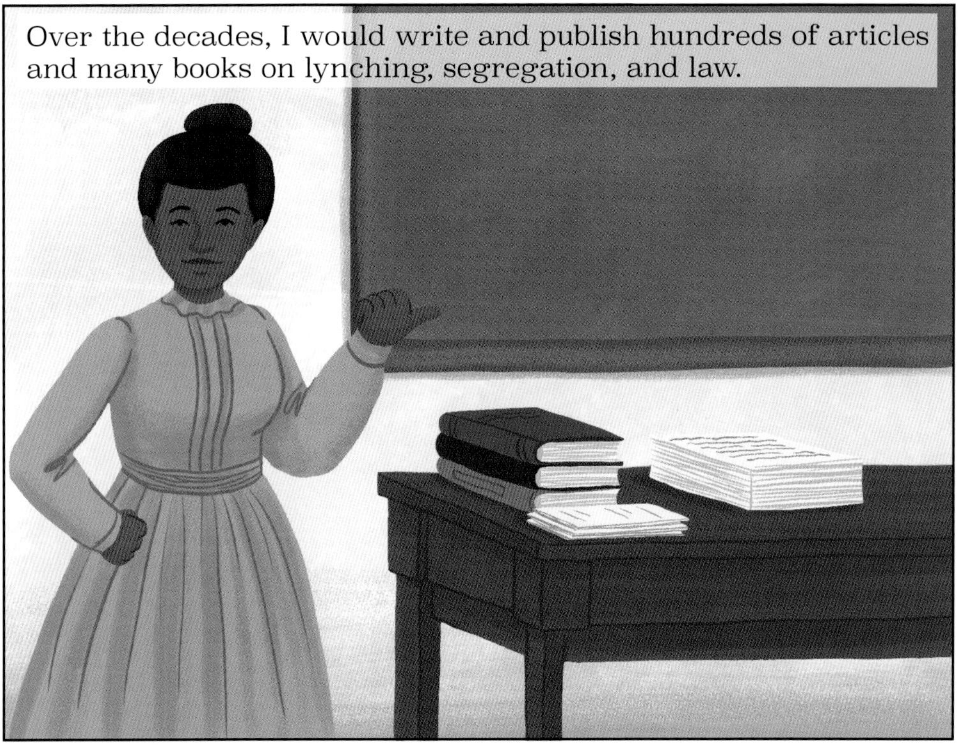
Over the decades, I would write and publish hundreds of articles and many books on lynching, segregation, and law.

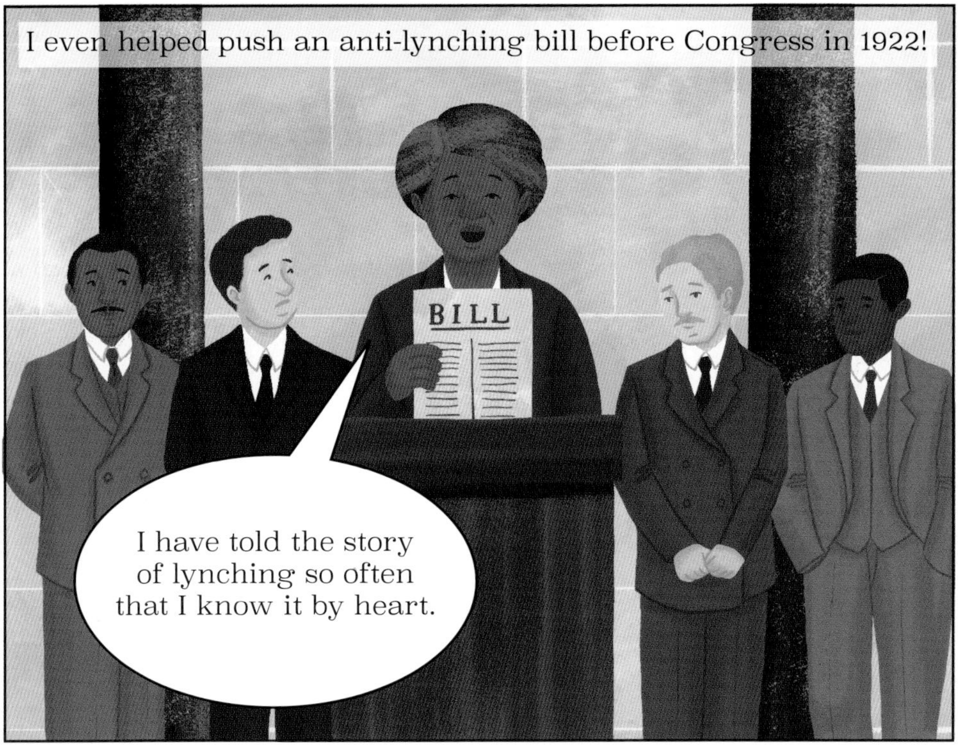
I even helped push an anti-lynching bill before Congress in 1922!
BILL
I have told the story of lynching so often that I know it by heart.

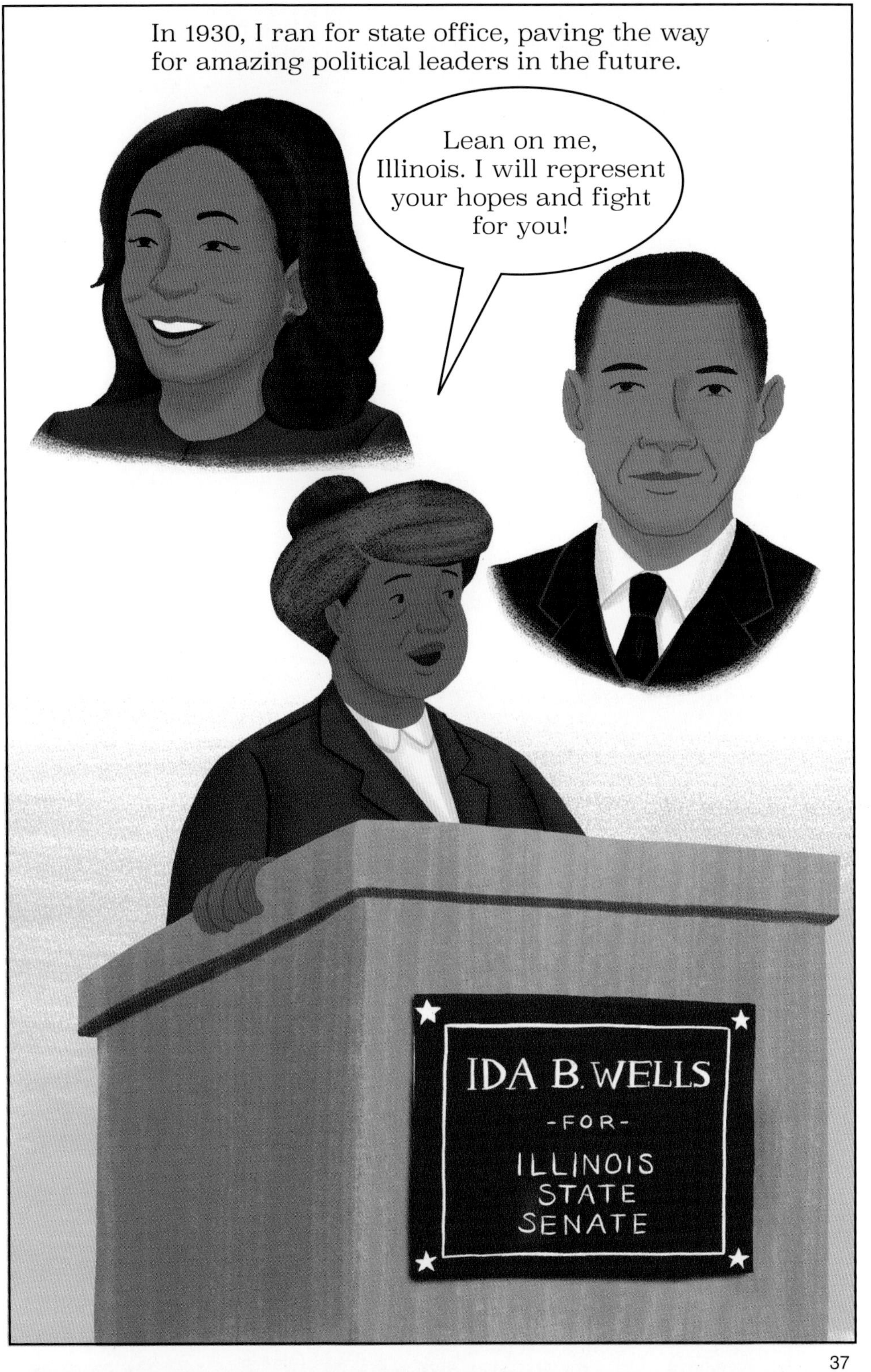
In 1930, I ran for state office, paving the way for amazing political leaders in the future.
Lean on me, Illinois. I will represent your hopes and fight for you!
IDA B. WELLS
-FOR-
ILLINOIS STATE SENATE

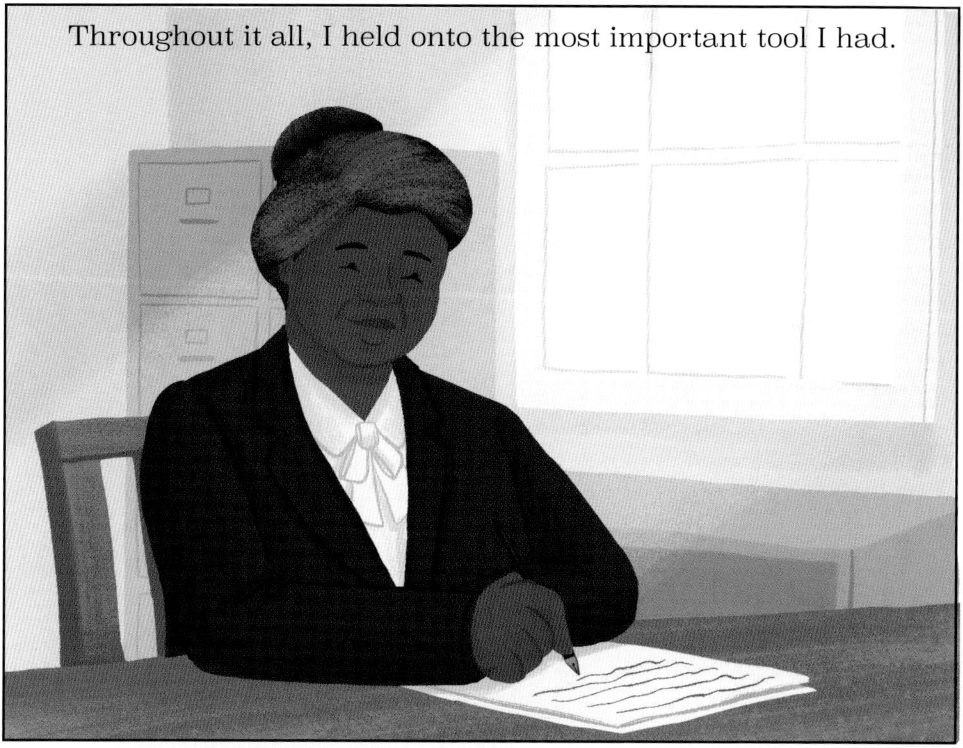
Throughout it all, I held onto the most important tool I had.

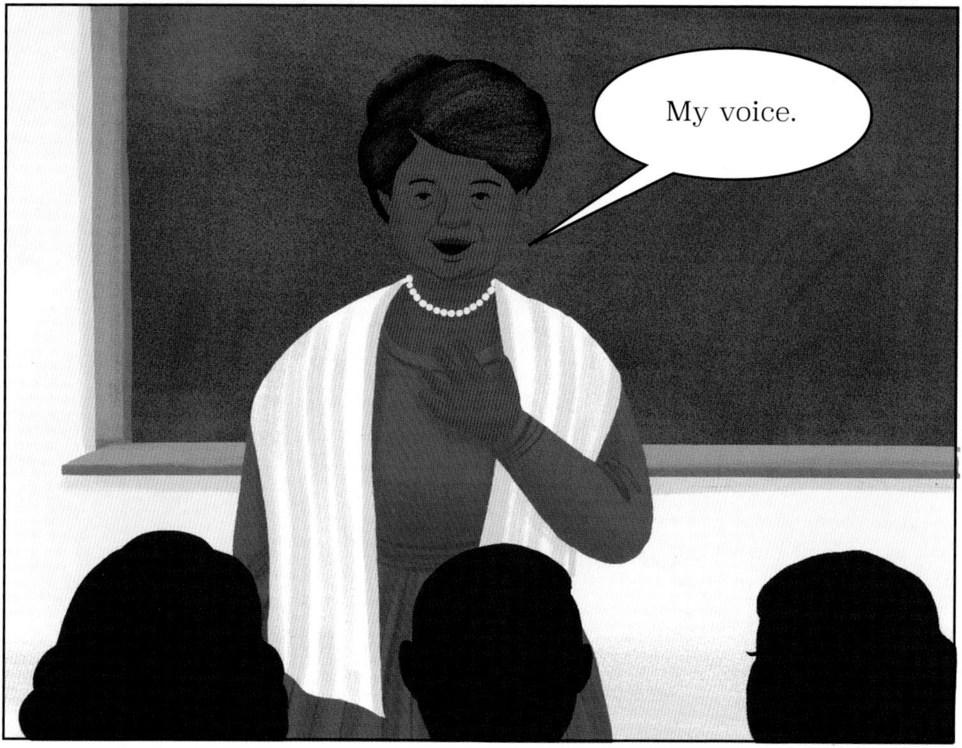
My voice.

In my lifetime, I saw changes that my father only dreamed of. And change continued long after my time.

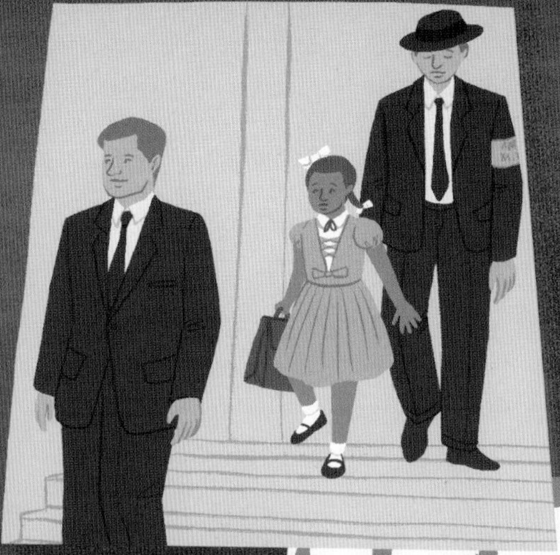

But, reader, my work is not done.

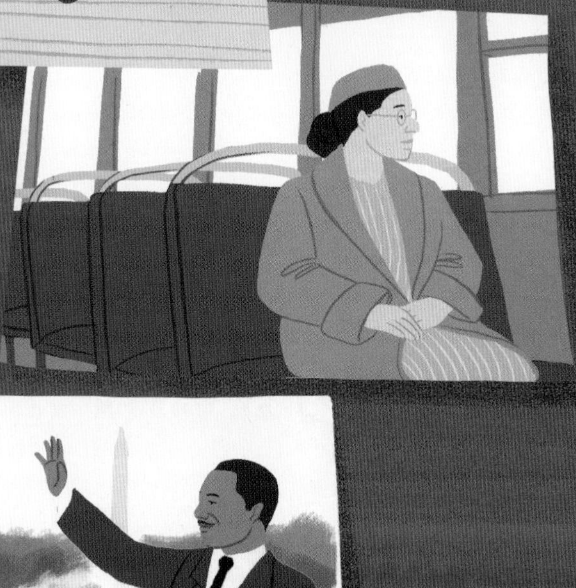

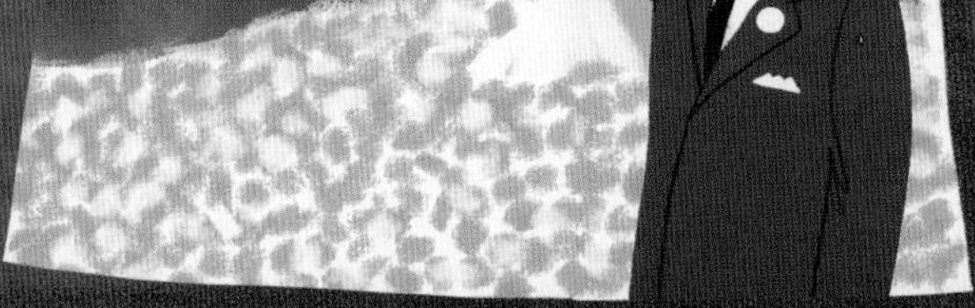

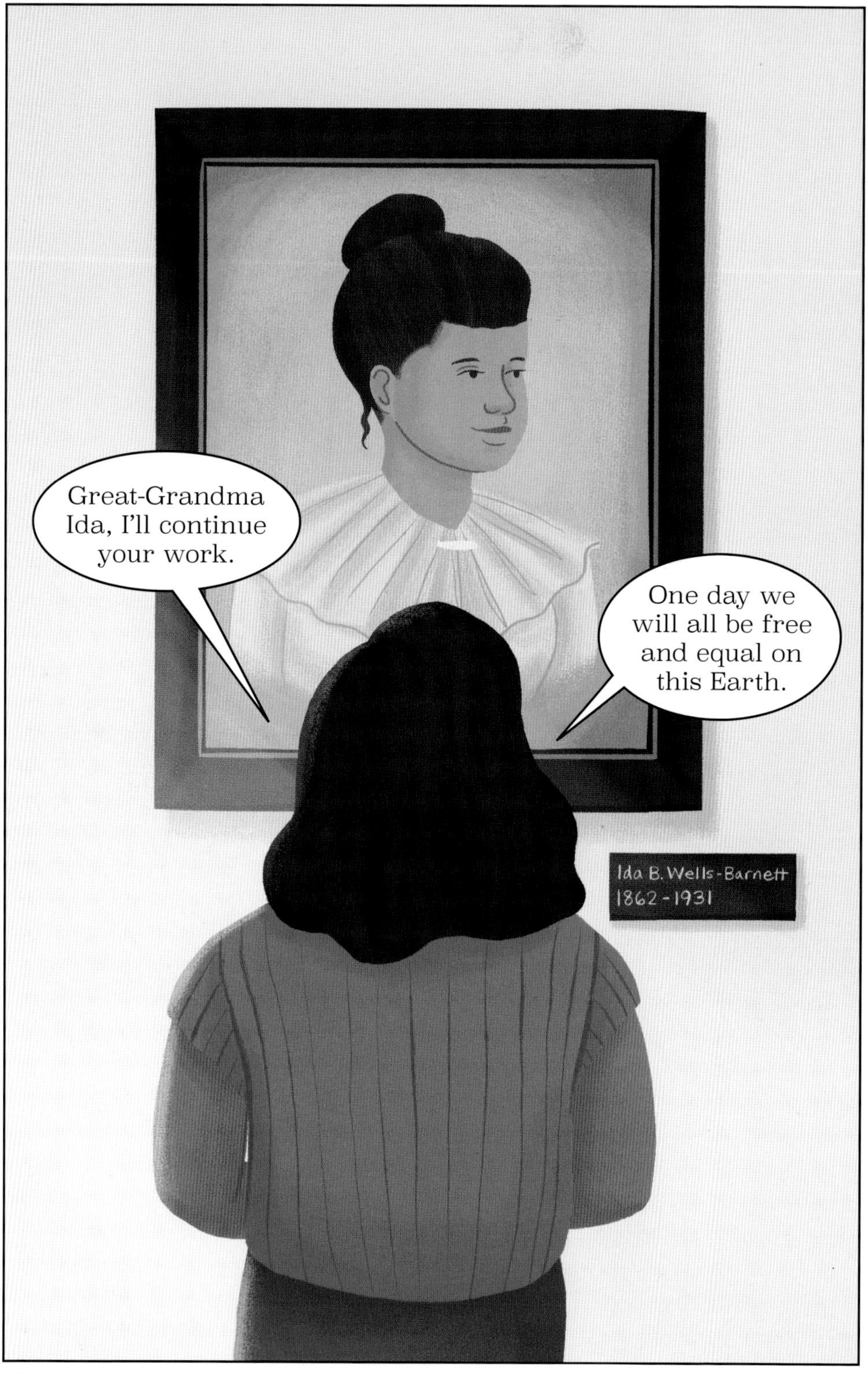
Great-Grandma Ida, I'll continue your work.
One day we will all be free and equal on this Earth.
Ida B. Wells-Barnett
1862-1931

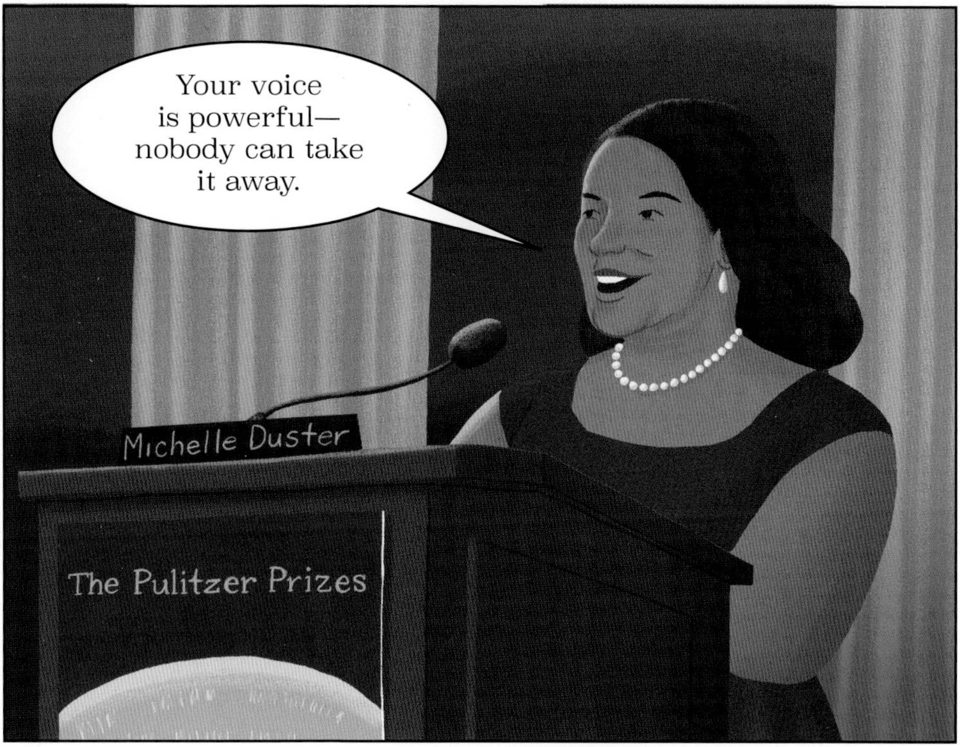
Your voice is powerful—nobody can take it away.
Michelle Duster
The Pulitzer Prizes

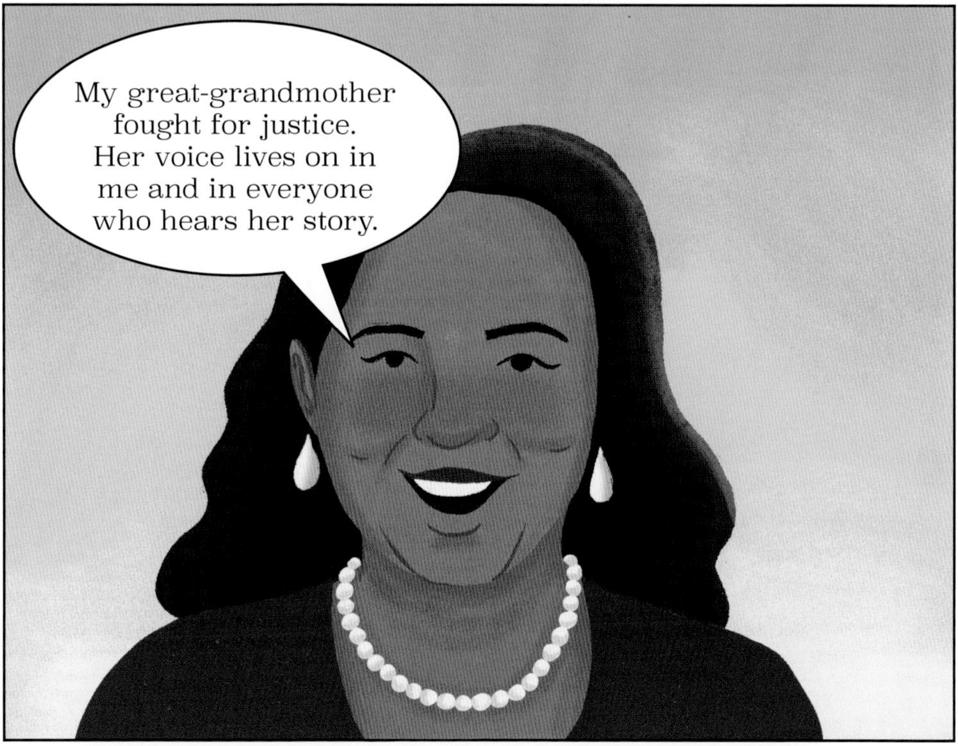
My great-grandmother fought for justice. Her voice lives on in me and in everyone who hears her story.

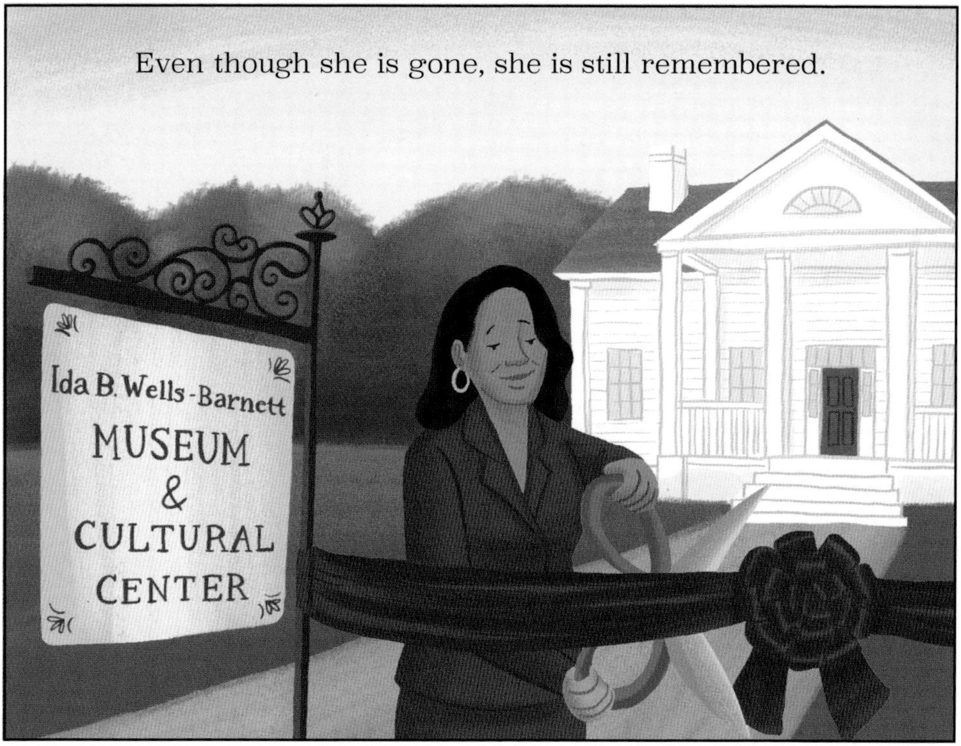
Even though she is gone, she is still remembered.
Ida B. Wells-Barnett
MUSEUM
&
CULTURAL
CENTER

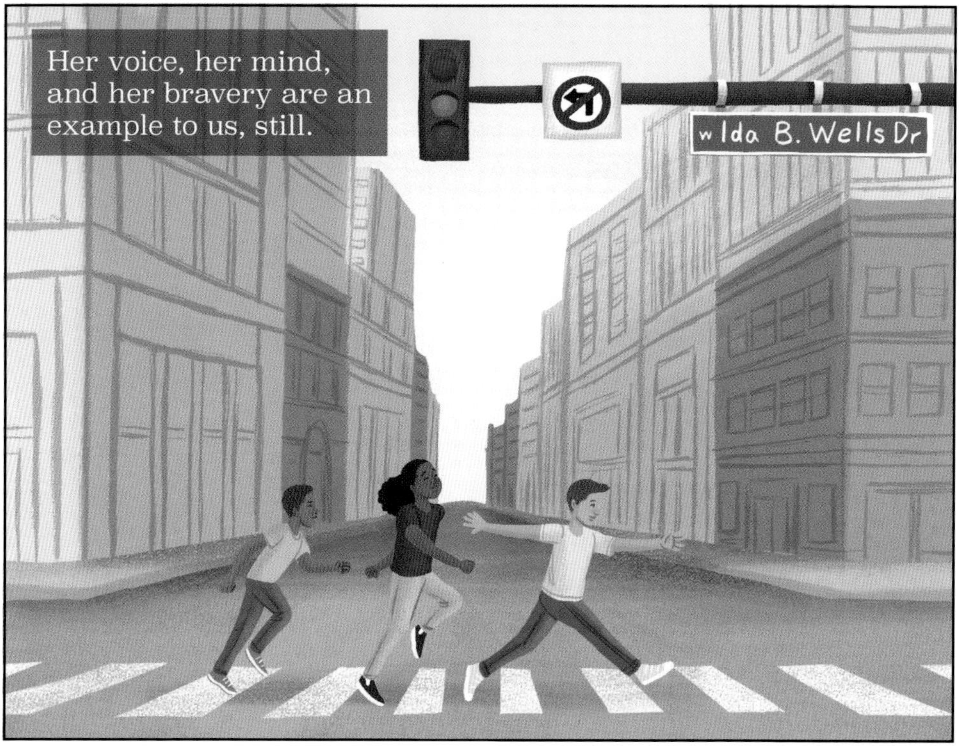
Her voice, her mind, and her bravery are an example to us, still.
W Ida B. Wells Dr

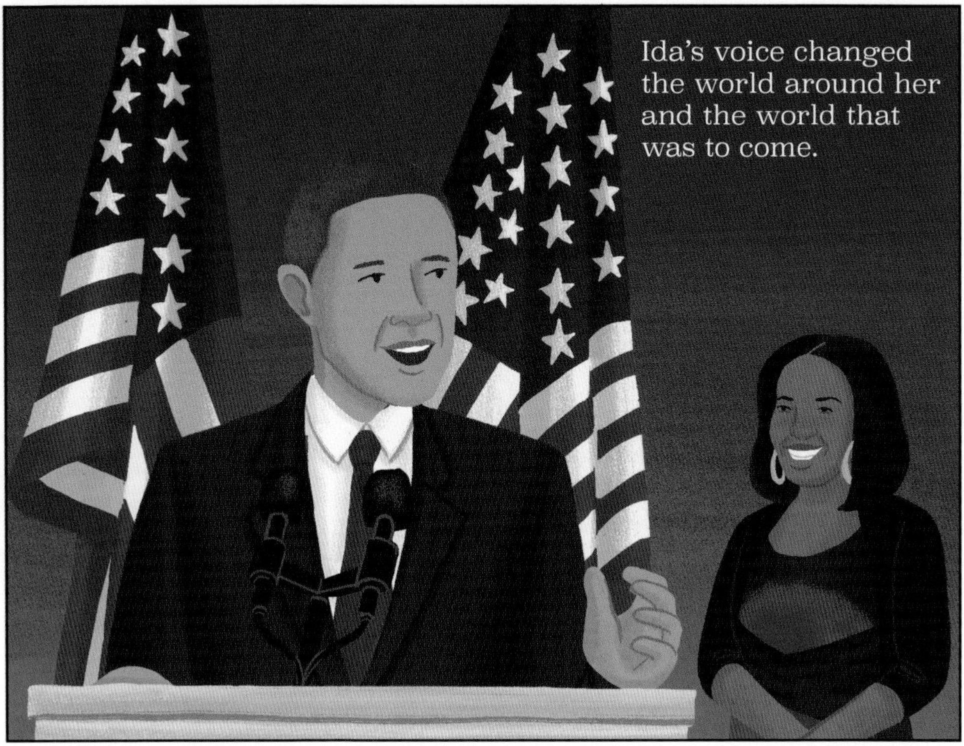
Ida's voice changed the world around her and the world that was to come.

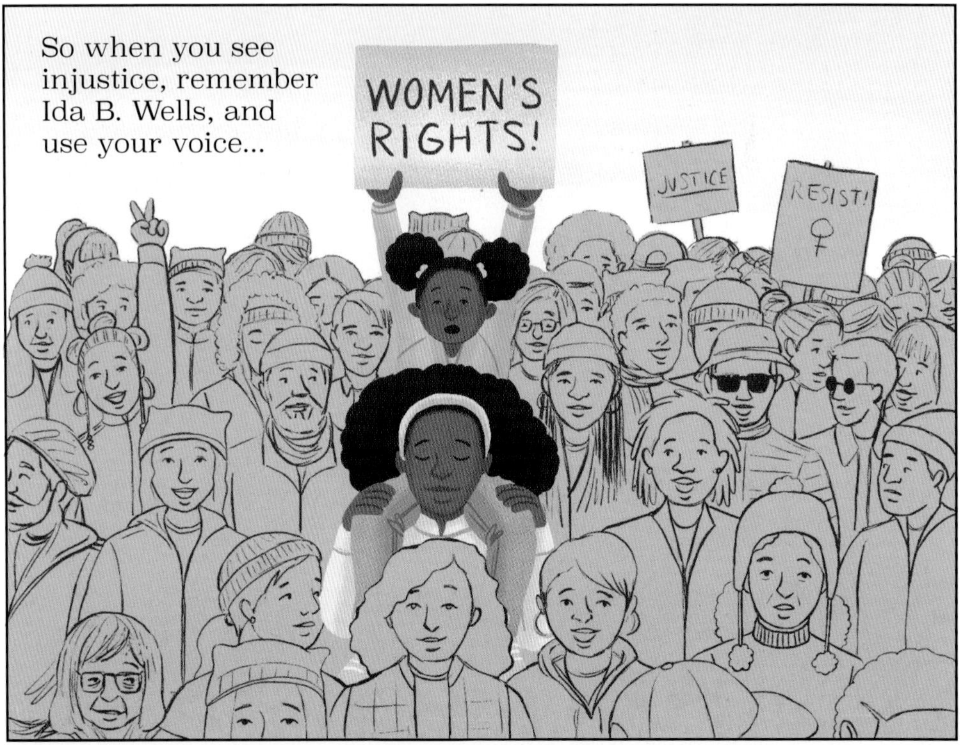
So when you see injustice, remember Ida B. Wells, and use your voice...
WOMEN'S RIGHTS!
JUSTICE
RESIST!

...to change our world.

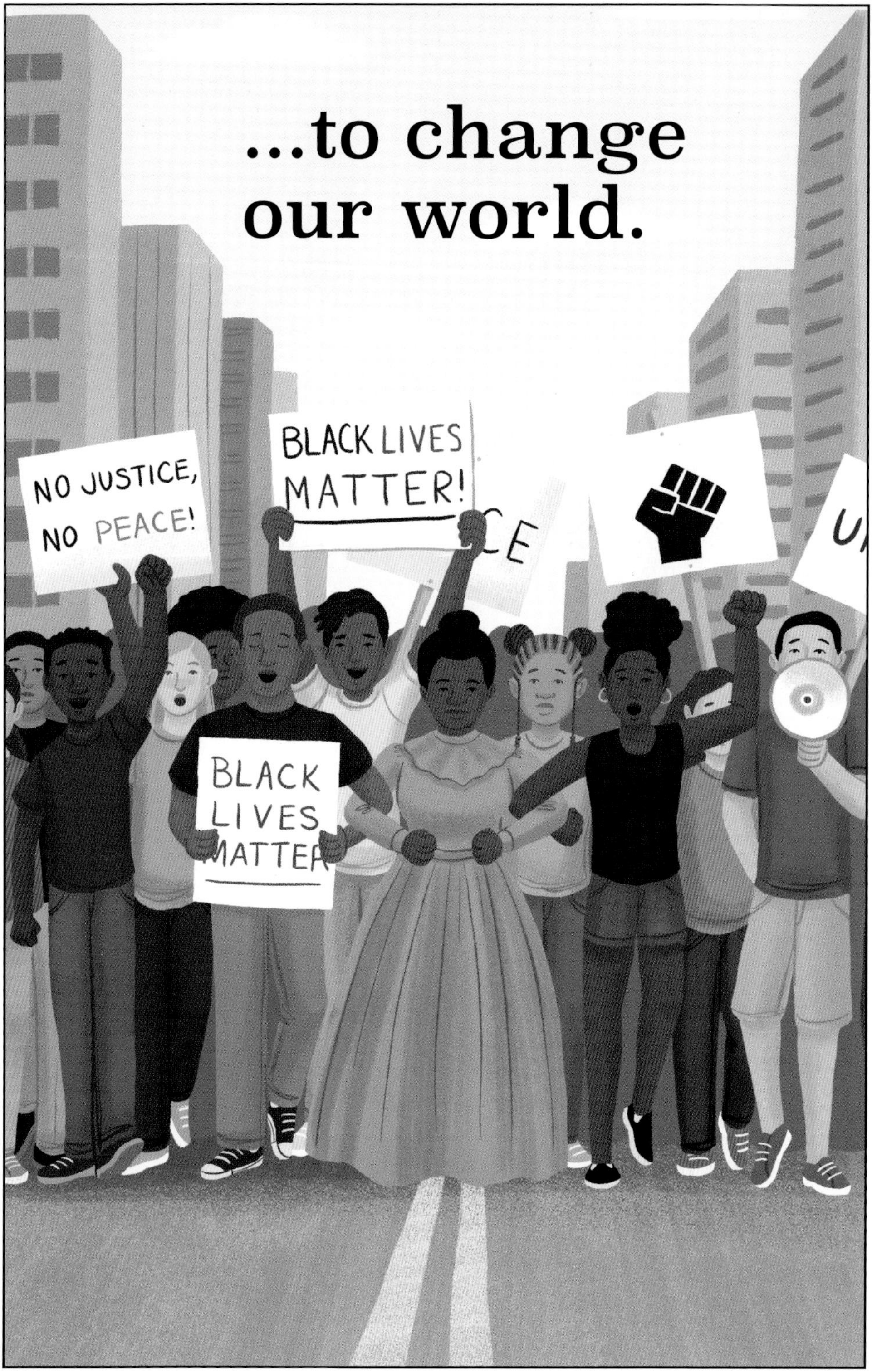
NO JUSTICE, NO PEACE!
BLACK LIVES MATTER!
BLACK LIVES MATTER

Anastasia Magloire Williams enjoys working with bold characters and writing vibrant stories that reflect a diverse and beautiful world. When she isn't reading everything in sight, she can be found tending to her many plants, gaming with her husband, or painting in her studio in sunny Florida.

Alleanna Harris is a graduate of the University of the Arts Animation program. She is inspired by the beauty in everyday things, such as how sunlight looks coming through the window in the morning or how people interact at the mall in her New Jersey town. In addition to illustrating, she likes listening to her favorite music playlists, sharing her art on Instagram, researching history articles, and hanging out with friends and family.

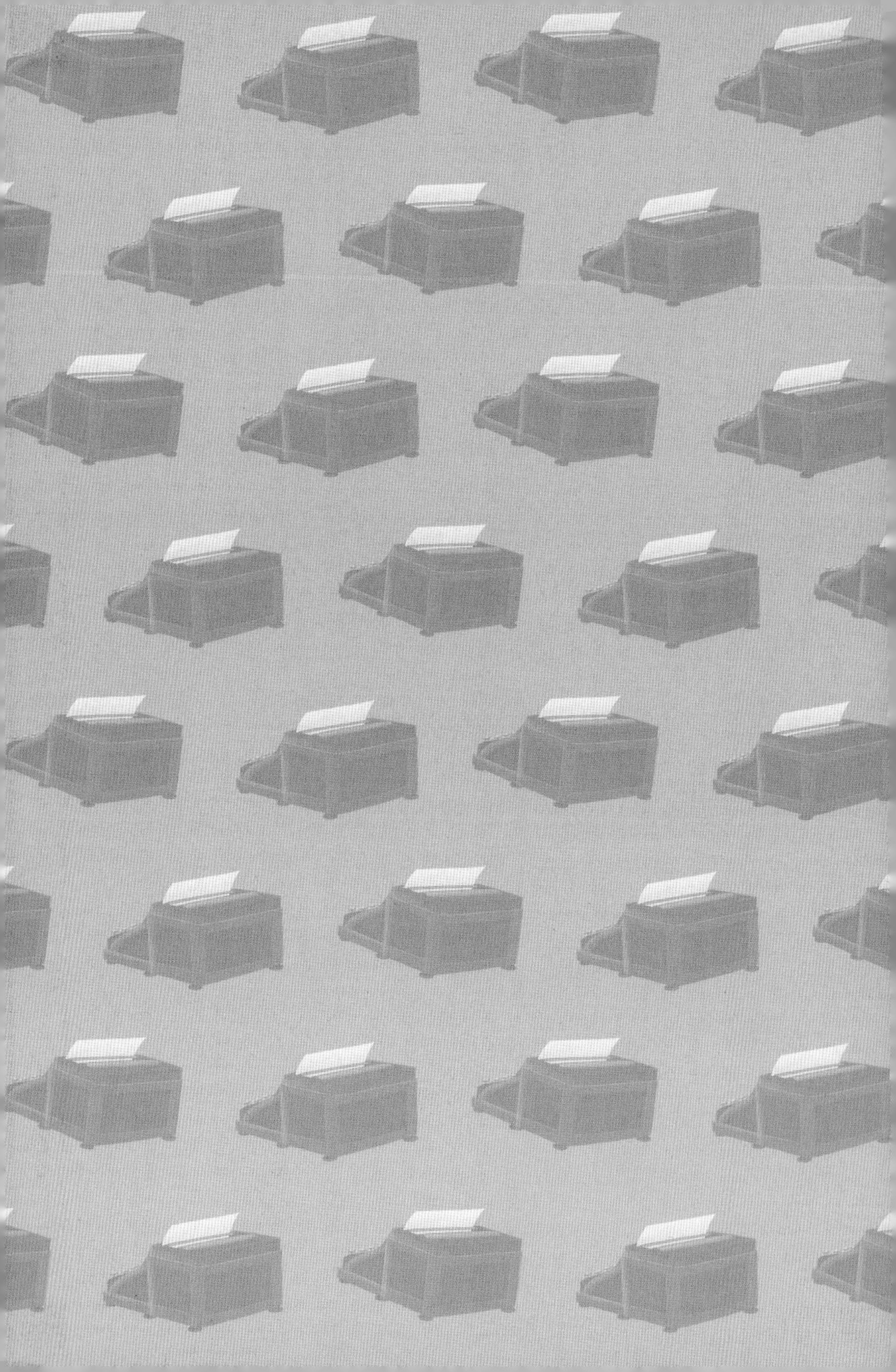